P9-CJL-009

BROADVIEW LIBRARY

NO LONGER PROPERTY OF
SEATTLE PUBLIC LIBRARY

LIBERALISM AND
ITS DISCONTENTS

Also by Francis Fukuyama

*Identity: The Demand for Dignity
and the Politics of Resentment*

*Political Order and Political Decay: From the Industrial
Revolution to the Globalization of Democracy*

*The Origins of Political Order: From Prehuman
Times to the French Revolution*

*America at the Crossroads: Democracy, Power,
and the Neoconservative Legacy*

*State-Building: Governance and World Order
in the Twenty-first Century*

*Our Posthuman Future:
Consequences of the Biotechnology Revolution*

*The Great Disruption: Human Nature
and the Reconstitution of Social Order*

Trust: The Social Virtues and the Creation of Prosperity

The End of History and the Last Man

LIBERALISM AND ITS DISCONTENTS

Francis Fukuyama

FARRAR, STRAUS AND GIROUX

NEW YORK

Farrar, Straus and Giroux
120 Broadway, New York 10271

Copyright © 2022 by Francis Fukuyama
All rights reserved
Printed in the United States of America
Originally published in 2022 by Profile Books Ltd., Great Britain
Published in the United States by Farrar, Straus and Giroux
First American edition, 2022

Library of Congress Cataloging-in-Publication Data
Names: Fukuyama, Francis, author.
Title: Liberalism and its discontents / Francis Fukuyama.
Description: First American edition. | New York : Farrar, Straus and
    Giroux, 2022.
Identifiers: LCCN 2021059692 | ISBN 9780374606718 (hardcover)
Subjects: LCSH: Liberalism. | Right and left (Political science)
Classification: LCC JC574 .F85 2022 | DDC 320.51—dc23/eng/20220206
LC record available at https://lccn.loc.gov/2021059692

Our books may be purchased in bulk for promotional,
educational, or business use. Please contact your local bookseller or
the Macmillan Corporate and Premium Sales Department at
1-800-221-7945, extension 5442, or by email at
MacmillanSpecialMarkets@macmillan.com.

www.fsgbooks.com
www.twitter.com/fsgbooks • www.facebook.com/fsgbooks

1   3   5   7   9   10   8   6   4   2

Contents

Preface

This book is intended to be a defense of classical liberalism, or, if that term is too fraught with certain historical connotations, then what Deirdre McCloskey labels "humane liberalism."[1] I believe that liberalism is under severe threat around the world today; while it was once taken for granted, its virtues need to be clearly articulated and celebrated once again.

By "liberalism," I refer to the doctrine that first emerged in the second half of the seventeenth century that argued for the limitation of the powers of governments through law and ultimately constitutions, creating institutions protecting the rights of individuals living under their jurisdiction. I do not refer to liberalism as it is used today in the United States as a label for left-of-center politics; that set of ideas, as we will see, has diverged from classical liberalism in certain critical ways. Nor does it refer to what in the United States is called libertarianism, which is a peculiar doctrine founded on hostility to government as such. I am not using liberal in the European sense either, where it designates center-right parties skeptical of socialism. Classical liberalism is a big tent that encompasses a range of political views that nonetheless agree on the foundational importance of equal individual rights, law, and freedom.

It is clear that liberalism has been in retreat in recent years. According to Freedom House, political rights and civil liberties around the world rose during the three and a half decades between 1974 and the early 2000s, but have been falling for fifteen straight years prior to 2021 in what has been labeled a democratic recession or even depression.[2]

In established liberal democracies, it is the liberal institutions that have come under immediate attack. Leaders like Hungary's Viktor Orbán, Poland's Jarosław Kaczyński, Brazil's Jair Bolsanaro, Turkey's Recep Tayyip Erdoğan, and America's Donald Trump were all legitimately elected, and have used their electoral mandates to attack liberal institutions in the first instance. These include the courts and justice system, nonpartisan state bureaucracies, independent media, and other bodies limiting executive power under a system of checks and balances. Orbán has been quite successful in packing the courts with his supporters and bringing the bulk of Hungarian media under the control of his allies. Trump was less successful in his attempts to weaken institutions like the Justice Department, the intelligence community, the courts, and the mainstream media, but his intention was much the same.

Liberalism has been challenged in recent years not just by populists of the right, but from a renewed progressive left as well. The critique from this quarter evolved from a charge—correct in itself—that liberal societies were not living up to their own ideals of equal treatment of all groups. This critique broadened over time to attack the underlying principles of liberalism itself, such as its positing of rights in individuals rather than groups, the premise of universal human equality on which constitutions and liberal rights have been based, and the value of free speech and scientific rationalism as methods of apprehending truth. In practice, this has led to intolerance of views that deviate from the new progressive orthodoxy, and the use of different forms of social and state power to enforce that orthodoxy. Dissident voices have been ousted from positions of influence and books effectively banned, often not by governments but by powerful organizations that control their mass distribution.

Populists on the right and progressives on the left are unhappy with present-day liberalism not, I would argue, because of a fundamental weakness in the doctrine. Rather, they are unhappy with the way that liberalism has evolved over the last couple of generations. Beginning in the late 1970s, economic liberalism evolved into what is now labeled neoliberalism, which dramatically increased economic inequality and brought on devastating financial crises that hurt ordinary people far more than wealthy elites in many countries around the globe. It is this inequality that is at the core of the progressive case against liberalism and the capitalist system with which it is associated. Liberalism's institutional rules protect the rights of everyone, including existing elites who are reluctant to give up either wealth or power, and who therefore stand as obstacles to the march towards social justice for excluded groups. Liberalism constituted the ideological basis for a market economy, and hence in the minds of many is implicated in the inequalities entailed by capitalism. Many impatient young Gen Z activists in America and Europe regard liberalism as an outmoded baby boomer perspective, a "system" that is incapable of reforming itself.

At the same time, the understanding of personal autonomy expanded relentlessly, and came to be seen as a value that trumped all other visions of the good life including those put forward by traditional religions and culture. Conservatives saw this as a threat to their most deeply held beliefs, and felt that they were being actively discriminated against by mainstream society. They felt that elites were using a host of undemocratic means—their control over the mainstream media, universities, the courts and executive power—to advance their agenda. The fact that conservatives won any number of elections in this period in the United States and Europe did not seem to make any difference in slowing the tidal wave of cultural change.

These discontents with the way that liberalism has evolved in recent decades have led to demands from both right and left that the doctrine be replaced root and branch by a different kind of system. On the right, there have been efforts to manipulate the electoral system in the United States in order to guarantee that conservatives remain in power, regardless of democratic choice; others have flirted with the use of violence and authoritarian government as a response to the threat they see. On the left, there are demands for a massive redistribution of wealth and power, as well as recognition of groups rather than individuals based on fixed characteristics such as race and gender, as well as policies to equalize outcomes between them. Since none of this is likely to happen on the basis of a broad social consensus, progressives are happy to continue to make use of courts, executive agencies, and their substantial social and cultural power to further this agenda.

These threats to liberalism are not symmetrical. The one coming from the right is more immediate and political; the one on the left is primarily cultural and therefore slower-acting. Both are driven by discontents with liberalism that do not have to do with the essence of the doctrine, but rather with the way in which certain sound liberal ideas have been interpreted and pushed to extremes. The answer to these discontents is not to abandon liberalism as such, but to moderate it.

The plan of this book is as follows. Chapter 1 will define liberalism, and put forward the three major historical justifications for it. Chapters 2 and 3 will look at how economic liberalism evolved into the more extreme form "neoliberalism" and provoked strong opposition and discontent with capitalism itself. Chapters 4 and 5 will examine how the basic liberal principle of personal autonomy was absolutized, and turned into a critique of the individualism and the universalism on which liberalism rested. Chapter 6 deals with the critique of modern natural science that was pioneered on the progressive left but soon spread to the populist right, while chapter 7 describes how modern technology has challenged the liberal principle of free speech. Chapter 8 questions whether either the right or left have viable alternatives to liberalism; chapter 9 looks at the challenge to liberalism posed by the need for national identity; and chapter 10 lays out the broad principles required to rebuild faith in classical liberalism.

I do not intend this book to be a history of liberal thought. There are dozens of important writers who have contributed to the liberal tradition, and there have been just as many critics of liberalism over the years as well.[3] There are hundreds if not thousands of books explicating their respective contributions. I want to focus instead on what I regard as the core ideas underlying contemporary liberalism, as well as some of the grave weaknesses afflicting liberal theory.

I am writing this book in a period when liberalism has faced numerous critiques and challenges, and appears to many people as an old and worn-out ideology that fails to answer the challenges of the times. This is hardly the first time it has been criticized. No sooner did liberalism become a living ideology in the wake of the French Revolution than it was attacked by Romantic critics who considered it to be based on a calculating and sterile worldview. It was further attacked by nationalists who, by the time of the First World War, had swept the field, and by the communists who opposed them. Outside of Europe, liberal doctrines sank roots in some societies like India, but were quickly challenged by nationalist, Marxist, and religious movements.

Nonetheless, liberalism survived these challenges and became the dominant organizing principle of much of world politics by the end of the twentieth century. Its durability reflects the fact that it has practical, moral, and economic justifications that appeal to many people, especially after they have been exhausted by the violent struggles engendered by alternative political systems. It is not, as Vladimir Putin suggested, an "obsolete" doctrine, but one that continues to be necessary in our present diverse and interconnected world. It is for that reason that it is necessary to restate the justifications for liberal politics, but also to articulate the reasons that many people today find it wanting.

Especially since 2016 there have been a plethora of books, articles, and manifestos analyzing liberalism's shortcomings and proffering advice on how liberalism needs to adapt to present circumstances.[4] I have spent a great deal of my life researching, teaching, and writing about public policy, and have no end of ideas about specific initiatives that could be undertaken to improve life in our contemporary liberal democracies. Rather than offering such a laundry list, however, the present volume will focus more narrowly on the basic principles that underlie a liberal regime, to expose some of their shortcomings, and, based on that, propose ways in which they could be addressed. Whatever the shortcomings, I want to show that they remain superior to the illiberal alternatives. I leave it to others to draw more specific policy conclusions from the general principles.

I would like to thank my UK publisher Andrew Franklin at Profile Books for pushing me to write this present volume. Andrew has published all nine of my previous books, and has been a tremendous editor and supporter over several decades. I would also like to thank my American editor Eric Chinski at Farrar, Straus and Giroux, who has provided invaluable advice on substance as well as style. My literary agents Esther Newberg, Karolina Sutton, and Sophie Baker have done their usual superb job in putting this book before wider audiences. In the fall of 2020 I worked with Jeff Gedmin and other colleagues to establish a new online journal, *American Purpose*, for which I wrote the lead essay on which this work is based.[5] That essay was intended to define the objectives of *American Purpose*, which hopefully will contribute to the political and ideological struggle in which we are now engaged. I would like to thank my colleagues and staff at that magazine, as well as Samuel Moyn, Shadi Hamid, Ian Bassin, Jeet Heer, Dhruva Jaishankar, Shikha Dalmia, Aaron Sibarium, Joseph Capizzi, and

Preface

Richard Thompson Ford for their comments on that original article. I would like to thank a number of people for their advice and comments, including Tara Isabella Burton, Gerhard Casper, Shikha Dalmia, Mark Cordover, David Epstein, Larry Diamond, Mathilde Fasting, David Fukuyama, Bill Galston, Jeff Gedmin, Erik Jensen, Yascha Mounk, Marc Plattner, and Abe Shulsky. Finally, I'd like to thank Ben Zuercher for his work as a research assistant.

1

What Is Classical Liberalism?

There are several broad characteristics that define liberalism, that distinguish it from other doctrines and political systems. In the words of John Gray,

> Common to all variants of the liberal tradition is a definite conception, distinctively modern in character, of man and society . . . It is *individualist*, in that it asserts the moral primacy of the person against the claims of any social collectivity; *egalitarian*, inasmuch as it confers on all men the same moral status and denies the relevance to legal or political order of differences in moral worth among human beings; *universalist*, affirming the moral unity of the human species and according a secondary importance to specific historic associations and cultural forms; and *meliorist* in its affirmation of the corrigibility and improvability of all social institutions and political arrangements. It is this conception of man and society which gives liberalism a definite identity which transcends its vast internal variety and complexity.[1]

Liberal societies confer rights on individuals, the most fundamental of which is the right to autonomy, that is, the ability to make choices with regard to speech, association, belief, and ultimately political life. Included within the sphere of autonomy is the right to own property and to undertake economic transactions. Over time, autonomy would also come to include the right to a share of political power through the right to vote.

Needless to say, early liberals had a restricted understanding of who qualified as a rights-bearing human being. This circle was initially limited, in the United States and other "liberal" regimes, to white men who owned property, and only later was broadened to other social groups. Nonetheless, these restrictions on rights ran contrary to the assertions of human equality contained both in the doctrinal writings of liberal theorists like Thomas Hobbes and John Locke, and in foundational documents like the US Declaration of Independence or the French Revolution's Declaration of the Rights of Man and of the Citizen. The tension between theory and practice drove, as well as the grass-roots mobilization of excluded groups, the evolution of liberal regimes towards a broader and more inclusive recognition of human equality. In this manner, liberalism differed sharply a manner that differed sharply from nationalist or religiously based doctrines that explicitly limited rights to certain races, ethnicities, genders, confessions, castes, or status groups.

Liberal societies embed rights in formal law, and as a result tend to be highly procedural. Law is simply a system of explicit rules that define how conflicts are to be resolved and collective decisions made, embodied in a set of legal institutions that function semi-autonomously from the rest of the political system so that it cannot be abused by politicians for short-term advantage. These rules have become progressively more complex over time in most advanced liberal societies.

Liberalism is often subsumed under the term "democracy," though strictly speaking liberalism and democracy are based on distinct principles and institutions. Democracy refers to rule by the people, which today is institutionalized in periodic free and fair multiparty elections under universal adult suffrage. Liberalism in the sense I am using it refers to the rule of law, a system of formal rules that restrict the powers of the executive, even if that executive is democratically legitimated through an election. Thus we should properly refer to "liberal democracy" when we talk about the type of regime that has prevailed in North America, Europe, parts of East and South Asia, and elsewhere in the world since the end of the Second World War. The United States, Germany, France, Japan, and India were all established as liberal democracies by the second half of the twentieth century, although some, like the United States and India, have been backsliding in the last few years.

It is liberalism rather than democracy that has come under the sharpest attack in recent years. Few people argue today that governments should not reflect the interests of "the people," and even overtly autocratic regimes like those in China or North Korea claim to be acting on their behalf. Vladimir Putin still feels compelled to hold regular "elections" and seems to care about popular support, as do many other de facto authoritarian leaders around the world. On the other hand, Putin has said that liberalism is an "obsolete doctrine,"[2] and has been working hard to silence critics, jail, kill, or harass opponents, and eliminate any independent civic space. China's Xi Jinping has attacked the idea that there should be any constraints on the power of the Communist Party, and has tightened its grip on every aspect of Chinese society. Hungary's Viktor Orbán has explicitly said that he is seeking to build an "illiberal democracy" in the heart of the European Union.[3]

When liberal democracy regresses, it is the liberal institutions that act as the canaries in the coal mine for the broader authoritarian assault to come. Liberal institutions protect the democratic process by limiting executive power; once they are eroded, democracy itself comes under attack. Electoral outcomes can then be manipulated through gerrymandering, voter qualification rules, or false charges of electoral fraud. The enemies of democracy guarantee that they will remain in power, regardless of the will of the people. Of Donald Trump's many assaults on American institutions, the most serious by far was his unwillingness to concede his loss of the 2020 presidential election and to peacefully transfer power to his successor.

Normatively, I believe that both liberalism and democracy are morally justified and necessary as a matter of practical politics. They constitute two of the three pillars of proper government, and both are critical as constraints on the third pillar, the modern state—a point I elaborated at some length in my *Political Order* series.[4] However, the present-day crisis of liberal democracy revolves in the first instances less around democracy strictly understood than around liberal institutions. Further, it is liberalism much more than democracy that is associated with economic growth and the prosperity of the modern world. As we will see in chapters 2 and 3, economic growth detached from considerations of equality and justice can be very problematic, but growth remains a necessary precondition for most of the other good things that societies seek.

There have been three essential justifications for liberal societies put forward over the centuries. The first is a pragmatic rationale: liberalism is a way of regulating violence and allowing diverse populations to live peacefully with one another. The second is moral: liberalism protects basic human dignity, and in particular human autonomy—the ability of each individual to make choices. The final justification is economic: liberalism promotes economic growth and all the good things that come from growth, by protecting property rights and the freedom to transact.

Liberalism has a strong association with certain forms of cognition, particularly the scientific method, which is seen as the best means of understanding and manipulating the external world. Individuals are assumed to be the best judges of their own interests, and are able to take in and test empirical information about the outside world in the making of those judgments. While judgments will necessarily vary, there is a liberal belief that in a free marketplace of ideas, good ideas will in the end drive out bad ones through deliberation and evidence.

The pragmatic argument for liberalism needs to be understood in the historical context in which liberal ideas first arose. The doctrine appeared in the middle of the seventeenth century towards the conclusion of Europe's wars of religion, a 150-year period of almost continuous violence that was triggered by the Protestant Reformation. It is estimated that as much as one-third of central Europe's population died in the course of the Thirty Years' War, if not from direct violence then from the famine and disease that followed upon military conflict. Europe's religious wars were driven by economic and social factors, such as the greed of monarchs eager to seize Church property. But they derived their ferocity from the fact that the warring parties represented different Christian sects that wanted to impose their particular interpretation of religious dogma on their populations. Martin Luther struggled with the emperor Charles V; the Catholic League fought the Huguenots in France; Henry VIII sought to separate the Church of England from Rome; and there were conflicts within the Protestant and Catholic camps between high and low church Anglicans, Zwinglians and Lutherans, and many others. This was a period in which heretics were regularly burned at the stake or drawn and quartered for professing belief in things like "transubstantiation," a level of cruelty that is hardly understandable as an outgrowth of economic motives alone.

Liberalism sought to lower the aspirations of politics, not as a means of seeking the good life as defined by religion, but rather as a way of ensuring life itself, that is, peace and security. Thomas Hobbes, writing in the middle of the English Civil War, was a monarchist, but he saw a strong state primarily as a guarantee that mankind would not return to the war of "every man against every man." The fear of violent death was, according to him, the most powerful passion, one that was universally shared by human beings in a way that religious beliefs were not. Therefore the first duty of the state was to protect the right to life. This was the distant origin of the phrase "*life*, liberty, and the pursuit of happiness" in the US Declaration of Independence. Building on this foundation, John Locke observed that life could also be threatened by a tyrannical state, and that the state itself needed to be constrained by the "consent of the governed."

Classical liberalism can therefore be understood as an institutional solution to the problem of governing over diversity, or, to put it in slightly different terms, of peacefully managing diversity in pluralistic societies. The most fundamental principle enshrined in liberalism is one of tolerance: you do not have to agree with your fellow citizens about the most important things, but only that each individual should get to decide what they are without interference from you or from the state. Liberalism lowers the temperature of politics by taking questions of final ends off the table: you can believe what you want, but you must do so in private life and not seek to impose your views on your fellow citizens.

The kinds of diversity that liberal societies can successfully manage are not unlimited. If a significant part of a society does not accept liberal principles themselves and seeks to restrict the fundamental rights of other people, or when citizens resort to violence to get their way, then liberalism is not sufficient to maintain political order. That was the situation in the United States prior to 1861 when the country was riven by the issue of slavery, and why it subsequently fell into civil war. During the Cold War, liberal societies in Western Europe faced similar threats from Eurocommunist parties in France and Italy, and in the contemporary Middle East the prospects for liberal democracy have suffered due to the strong suspicion that Islamist parties like the Muslim Brotherhood in Egypt do not accept the liberal rules of the game.

Diversity can take many forms: in seventeenth-century Europe it was religious, but it can also be based on nationality, ethnicity, race, or other types of belief. Byzantine society was riven by a sharp polarization between the Blues and Greens, racing teams in the Hippodrome that corresponded to Christian sects professing belief in Monophysite and Monothelite doctrines respectively. Poland today is one of the most ethnically and religiously homogeneous societies in Europe, and yet it is sharply polarized between social groups based in its cosmopolitan cities and a more conservative one in the countryside. Human beings are very good at dividing themselves into teams that go to war with one another metaphorically or literally; diversity thus is a prevalent characteristic of many human societies.[5]

Liberalism's most important selling point remains the pragmatic one that existed in the seventeenth century: if diverse societies like India or the United States move away from liberal principles and try to base national identity on race, ethnicity, religion, or some other substantive vision of the good life, they are inviting a return to potentially violent conflict. The United States suffered such conflict during its Civil War, and Modi's India is inviting communal violence by shifting its national identity to one based on Hinduism.

The second justification for a liberal society is a moral one: a liberal society protects human dignity by granting citizens an equal right to autonomy. The ability to make fundamental life choices is a critical human characteristic. Every individual wants to determine their life's goals: what they will do for a living, whom they will marry, where they will live, with whom they will associate and transact, what and how they should speak, and what they will believe. It is this freedom that gives human beings dignity, and unlike intelligence, physical appearance, skin color, or other secondary characteristics, it is universally shared by all human beings. At a minimum, the law protects autonomy by granting and enforcing citizens' rights to speak, associate, and believe. But over time autonomy has come to encompass the right to have a share in political power and to participate in self-government through the right to vote. Liberalism has thus become tied to democracy, which can be seen as an expression of collective autonomy.

The view of liberalism as a means of protecting basic human dignity that emerged in Europe by the time of the French Revolution has now been written into countless constitutions of liberal democracies around the world in the form of the "right to dignity," and appears in the basic laws of countries as diverse as Germany, South Africa, and Japan. Most contemporary politicians would be hard-pressed to explain precisely which human qualities give people equal dignity, but they would have a vague sense that it implies something about the capacity for choice, and the ability to make decisions about one's own life course without undue interference from governments or broader society.

Liberal theory asserted that these rights applied to all human beings universally, as in the Declaration of Independence's opening phrase "We hold these truths to be self-evident, that all men are created equal." But, in practice, liberal regimes made invidious distinctions between individuals, and did not regard all of the people under their jurisdiction as full human beings. The United States did not grant citizenship and the franchise to African Americans until passage of the Fourteenth, Fifteenth, and Sixteenth amendments in the wake of the Civil War, and after Reconstruction shamefully took them back in a period that stretched up to the Civil Rights era in the 1960s. And the country did not grant women the right to vote until passage of the Nineteenth Amendment in 1919. Similarly, European democracies opened up the franchise to all adults only gradually, removing restrictions based on property ownership, gender, and race in a slow process that stretched into the middle of the twentieth century.[6]

The third major justification for liberalism had to do with its connection to economic growth and modernization. For many nineteenth-century liberals, the most important form of autonomy was the ability to buy, sell, and invest freely in a market economy. Property rights were central to the liberal agenda, along with contract enforcement through institutions that lowered the risk of trade and investment with strangers. The theoretical justification for this is clear: no entrepreneur will risk money in a business if he or she thinks that it will be expropriated the following year either by a government, business competitors, or a criminal organization. Property rights needed to be supported by a large legal apparatus that included a system of independent courts, lawyers, a bar, and a state that could use its police powers to enforce judgments against private parties.

Liberal theory did not only endorse the freedom to buy and sell within national borders; early on it argued in favor of an international system of free trade. Adam Smith's 1776 *Wealth of Nations* demonstrated the ways in which mercantilist restrictions on trade (for example, the Spanish Empire's requirement that Spanish goods be carried only in Spanish ships to Spanish ports) were highly inefficient. David Ricardo laid the basis for modern trade theory with his theory of comparative advantage. Liberal regimes did not necessarily follow these theoretical dictates: both Britain and the United States, for example, protected their early industries with tariffs, until the point where they grew to a scale that allowed them to compete without government assistance. Nonetheless, there has been a strong historical association between liberalism and freedom of commerce.

Property rights were among the initial rights to be guaranteed by rising liberal regimes, well before the right to associate or vote. The first two European countries to establish strong property rights were England and the Netherlands, both of which developed an entrepreneurial commercial class and saw explosive economic growth. In North America, English common law protected property rights prior to the time when the colonies gained their political independence. The German *Rechtsstaat*, building on civil codes like Prussia's 1792 *Allgemeines Landrecht*, protected private property long before the German lands saw a hint of democracy. Like America, autocratic but liberal Germany industrialized rapidly in the late nineteenth century and had become an economic great power by the early twentieth century.

The connection between classical liberalism and economic growth is not a trivial one. Between 1800 and the present, output per person in the liberal world grew nearly 3,000 percent.[7] These gains were felt up and down the economic ladder, with ordinary workers enjoying levels of health, longevity, and consumption unavailable to the most privileged elites in earlier ages.

The central place of property rights in liberal theory meant that the strongest advocates of liberalism tended to be the new middle classes that were the by-product of economic modernization—what Karl Marx would call the bourgeoisie. The original backers of the French Revolution who took the Tennis Court Oath in 1789 were mostly middle-class lawyers who wanted to protect their property rights against the monarchy, and had little interest in extending the vote to the sans-culottes. The same was true of the American Founding Fathers, who almost universally came from a prosperous class of merchants and planters. James Madison argued in his "Address at the Virginia Convention" that "the rights of persons, and the rights of property, are the objects, for the protection of which Government was instituted." In his essay "Federalist 10", he noted that social classes and inequality would inevitably result from the necessary protection of property: "From the protection of different and unequal faculties of acquiring property, the possession of different degrees and kinds of property immediately results; and from the influence of these on the sentiments and views of the respective proprietors ensues a division of the society into different interests and parties."[8]

Liberalism's current travails are not new; the ideology has gone in and out of fashion over the centuries but has always returned because of its underlying strengths. It was born out of religious conflict in Europe; the principle that states should not seek to impose their sectarian views on others served to stabilize the Continent in the period after the Peace of Westphalia in 1648. Liberalism was one of the early driving forces of the French Revolution, and was initially an ally of democratic forces that wanted to expand political participation beyond the narrow circle of upper- and middle-class elites. The partisans of equality, however, broke with the partisans of liberty, and created a revolutionary dictatorship that ultimately gave way to the new empire under Napoleon. The latter, nonetheless, played a critical role in spreading liberalism in the form of law—the Code Napoléon—to the far corners of Europe. This then became the anchor for a liberal rule of law on the Continent.

Following the French Revolution, liberals were shunted aside by other doctrines on the right and on the left. The Revolution spawned the next major competitor to liberalism, which was nationalism. Nationalists argued that political jurisdictions should correspond to cultural units, defined largely by language and ethnicity. They rejected liberalism's universalism, and sought to confer rights primarily on their favored group. As the nineteenth century progressed, Europe reorganized itself from a dynastic basis to a national one, with the unification of Italy and Germany and growing nationalist agitation within the multiethnic Ottoman and Austro-Hungarian empires. In 1914 this exploded into the Great War, which killed millions of people and paved the way for a second global conflagration in 1939.

The defeat of Germany, Italy, and Japan in 1945 laid the basis for a restoration of liberalism as the democratic world's governing ideology. Europeans saw the folly of organizing politics around an exclusive and aggressive understanding of nation, and created the European Community and later the European Union to deliberately subordinate the old nation-states to a cooperative transnational structure.

Liberty for individuals necessarily implied liberty for the colonial peoples conquered by the European powers, leading to rapid collapse of their overseas empires. In some cases, colonies were granted independence voluntarily; in others, the metropolitan power resisted national liberation by force.

This process was completed only with the collapse of Portugal's overseas empire in the early 1970s. For its part, the United States played a powerful role in creating a new set of international institutions, including the United Nations (and affiliated Bretton Woods organizations like the World Bank and the International Monetary Fund), the General Agreement on Trade and Tariffs, its successor the World Trade Organization, and cooperative regional ventures like the North American Free Trade Agreement. American military power and commitments to the North Atlantic Treaty Organization and a series of bilateral alliance treaties with countries like Japan and South Korea undergirded a global security system that stabilized both Europe and East Asia during the Cold War.

The other major competitor to liberalism was communism. Liberalism is allied to democracy through its protection of individual autonomy, which implies juridical equality and a broad right to political choice and the franchise. But, as Madison observed, liberalism does not lead to an equality of outcomes, and from the French Revolution onwards there were strong tensions between liberals committed to the protection of property rights, and a left that sought redistribution of wealth and income through a strong state. In democratic countries this took the form of socialist or social democratic parties based on a rising labor movement like the Labour Party in Britain or the German Social Democrats. But the more radical proponents of democratic equality organized under the banner of Marxism–Leninism, and were willing to abandon liberal rule of law altogether and vest power in a dictatorial state.

The largest threat to the liberal international order that

took shape after 1945 came from the former Soviet Union, and its allied communist parties in Eastern Europe and East Asia. Aggressive nationalism may have been defeated in Europe, but it became a powerful source of mobilization in the developing world, and received backing from the USSR, China, Cuba, and other communist states. But the former Soviet Union collapsed between 1989 and 1991, and along with it the perceived legitimacy of Marxism–Leninism. China under Deng Xiaoping took a turn towards a market economy and sought to integrate itself into the burgeoning liberal international order, as did many former communist countries that joined existing international institutions like the European Union and NATO.

The late twentieth century thus saw a broad and largely happy coexistence of liberalism and democracy throughout the developed world. The liberal commitment to property rights and the rule of law laid the basis for the strong post–Second World War economic growth. Liberalism's pairing with democracy tempered the inequalities created by market competition, and general prosperity enabled democratically elected legislatures to create redistributive welfare states. Inequality was kept under control and made tolerable because most people could see their material conditions improving. The progressive immiseration of the proletariat foreseen by Marxism never occurred; rather, working-class people saw their incomes rise and turned from being opponents to supporters of the system. The period from 1950 to the 1970s—what the French call *les trente glorieuses*—was thus the heyday of liberal democracy in the developed world.

This was not just a period of economic growth, but one of increasing social equality. A whole series of social movements sprang up in the 1960s, beginning with the civil rights and feminist revolutions that pressured societies to live up to their liberal principles of universal human dignity. Communist societies pretended that they had solved problems related to race and gender, but in Western liberal democracies the social transformation was driven by grassroots mobilization rather than top-down decree and hence proved more thoroughgoing. The circle of rights-bearing individuals in liberal societies continued to expand, in a process that is incomplete and that continues up to the present day.

If one needed proof of liberalism's positive impact as an ideology, one should look no further than the success of a series of states in Asia that went from being impoverished developing countries to developed ones in a matter of decades. Japan, South Korea, Taiwan, Hong Kong, and Singapore were not democracies during their high-growth periods, but they adopted key liberal institutions like protection of private property rights and openness to international trade in ways that allowed them to take advantage of the global capitalist system. The reforms instituted by Deng Xiaoping in China after 1978, such as the Household Responsibility law or the township and village enterprise system, replaced central planning with limited property rights and incentives for peasants and entrepreneurs to take risks because they were allowed to enjoy the fruits of their own labor. There is a large literature explaining how the countries of East Asia never adopted anything like the full-blown form of market capitalism that existed in the United States—indeed, European capitalism looked very different as well.[9] In East Asia and in Europe, the state remained a much more important actor in encouraging economic growth than in the United States. But such "developmental states" still relied on liberal institutions like private property and incentives to trigger their remarkable records of economic growth.

Nonetheless, liberalism also had a number of short-comings, some of which were precipitated by external circumstances, and others of which were intrinsic to the doctrine. Most doctrines or ideologies begin with a core insight that is true or even revelatory, but they go wrong when that insight is carried to extremes—when the doctrine becomes, so to speak, doctrinaire.

Liberalism has seen its core principles pushed to extremes by advocates on both its right and left wings, to the point where those principles themselves were undermined. One of liberalism's core ideas is its valorization and protection of individual autonomy. But this basic value can be carried too far. On the right, autonomy meant primarily the right to buy and sell freely, without interference from the state. Pushing this notion to extremes, economic liberalism turned into "neoliberalism" in the late twentieth century and led to grotesque inequalities, which is the subject of the following two chapters. On the left, autonomy meant personal autonomy with regard to lifestyle choices and values, and resistance to the social norms imposed by the surrounding society. Pushed down this road, liberalism began to erode its own premise of tolerance as it evolved into modern identity politics. These extreme versions of liberalism then generated a backlash, which is the source of the right-wing populist and left-wing progressive movements that threaten liberalism today.

2

From Liberalism to Neoliberalism

One of the critical domains in which liberal ideas were taken to extremes lay in economic thought, where liberalism evolved into what has been labeled "neoliberalism."

Neoliberalism is often used today as a pejorative synonym for capitalism, but it should more properly be used in a narrower sense to describe a school of economic thought, often associated with the University of Chicago or the Austrian School, and economists like Milton Friedman, Gary Becker, George Stigler, Ludwig von Mises, and Friedrich Hayek, who sharply denigrated the role of the state in the economy, and emphasized free markets as spurs to growth and efficient allocators of resources. These economists, many of whom were awarded Nobel Prizes, provided a highbrow justification for the pro-market, anti-statist policies pursued by Ronald Reagan and Margaret Thatcher in the 1980s. These policies were continued by center-left politicians like Bill Clinton and Tony Blair, who promoted the deregulation and privatization of their economies in ways that laid the ground for the rise of populism in the late 2010s. This pro-market consensus was absorbed by a whole generation of young people, many of whom were subsequently disillusioned by the great financial crisis of 2008, the 2010 euro crisis, and subsequent economic travails.[1]

On a more popular level, neoliberalism was allied to what Americans label libertarianism, whose single underlying theme is hostility to an overreaching state and belief in the sanctity of individual freedom. Libertarians joined hands with Chicago-school economists in their hostility to state regulation of the economy, and their belief that governments would only get in the way of dynamic entrepreneurs and innovators. But their belief in the primacy of individual freedom led them to oppose state action in social matters as well. They were highly critical of the large and seemingly ever-expanding welfare states that had been created in most liberal democracies over the decades, and disapproved of state efforts to regulate personal behaviors like drug use and sexuality. Some libertarians believed it was simply up to individuals to take care of themselves. The more thoughtful ones argued that social needs could be better met through private action than through large state bureaucracies, whether by the private sector itself or in civil society (that is, non-profit organizations, churches, voluntary groups, and the like).

The Reagan-Thatcher neoliberal revolution was grounded in, and solved, some real problems. Economic policy in the developed world has swung between extremes over the past century and a half. The nineteenth century was the heyday of unregulated market capitalism, with state intervention playing little role in protecting individuals from a cutthroat form of capitalism, or dampening the impact of the recessions, depressions, and banking crises that occurred with great regularity.

This all changed by the early twentieth century. Beginning

in the 1880s, Progressive Era reformers put into place the foundations of a regulatory state, beginning in the United States with the Interstate Commerce Commission to regulate the railroads that were proliferating everywhere. The Sherman, Clayton, and Federal Trade Commission Acts gave the government powers to limit the growth of monopolies, and the severe banking crisis of 1908 led to the creation of the US Federal Reserve system. The Great Depression spawned a plethora of regulatory bodies like the Securities and Exchange Commission, as well as the Social Security Administration to organize pensions. The crisis of global capitalism in the 1930s gave states much greater legitimacy at the expense of private markets, leading to the rise of expansive regulatory and welfare states in Europe and North America.

By the 1970s, the pendulum had swung over to excessive state control. Many sectors of the economies of the United States and Europe were overregulated, and generous commitments to social welfare systems left many rich countries facing exploding debt loads. After experiencing nearly three decades of almost uninterrupted economic growth, the world economy hit a hard stop after the 1973 Middle East War and the quadrupling of oil prices by OPEC. Economic growth crawled to a halt and inflation soared around the world as the global economy tried to adjust to higher resource prices. The impact was most devastating in the developing world, where money center banks recycled oil-producing country surpluses into debt that countries in Latin America and sub-Saharan Africa used to maintain standards of living. This proved unsustainable; one country after another defaulted on their sovereign debts and experienced collapsing employment and hyperinflation. The cure for these problems undertaken by international financial institutions was that prescribed by the Chicago School: fiscal austerity, flexible exchange rates, deregulation, privatization, and strict control over domestic money supplies.

In the United States and other developed countries, deregulation and privatization had beneficial effects. The prices of airline tickets and trucking rates began to fall as states pulled back from the pervasive price controls they had imposed. Margaret Thatcher's most heroic moment was in her confrontation with Arthur Scargill and the coal-miners' union: Britain had no business mining coal at that point in its economic development, nor in owning companies like British Steel or British Telecom, which were more efficiently run by private operators. Britain's economic revival after a dismal decade, the 1970s, was due in large measure to neoliberal policies.

But the neoliberal agenda was pushed to a counterproductive extreme. A valid insight into the superior efficiency of markets evolved into something of a religion, in which state intervention was opposed as a matter of principle. Privatization was pushed, for example, even in cases of natural monopolies like key public utilities, leading to travesties like the privatization of Mexico's TelMex, where a public telecommunications monopoly was transformed into a private one and facilitated the rise of one of the world's richest men, Carlos Slim.

Some of the worst consequences were felt in the former Soviet Union, which fell apart right at the moment when neoliberal ideology was at its peak. Socialist central planning had been rightly discredited by the poor performance of communist economies all over the world. There was a belief among many economists, however, that private markets would form spontaneously once central planning was dismantled. They failed to understand that markets themselves function only when they are strictly regulated by states with functioning legal systems that have the capacity to enforce rules concerning transparency, contracts, ownership, and the like. As a result, large chunks of the Soviet economy were gobbled up by clever oligarchs whose malign influence continues to the present day in Russia, Ukraine, and other former communist countries.

Even as it promoted two decades of rapid economic growth, neoliberalism succeeded in destabilizing the global economy and undermining its own success. Deregulation was helpful in many sectors of the real economy, but proved disastrous when it was applied in the 1980s and 1990s to the financial sector. Former Federal Reserve chief Alan Greenspan and other economists at the time believed that the latter would be able to regulate itself. But financial institutions behave very differently from firms in the real economy. Unlike a manufacturing corporation, a large investment bank is systemically dangerous, and can impose huge costs on the economy as a whole if it takes excessive risks. This is what the world saw with the collapse of Lehman Brothers in September 2008, when thousands of counterparties around the world found themselves unable to meet their own obligations because of their entanglement with Lehman. The global payments system froze up and was rescued only by massive injections of liquidity by the US Federal Reserve and other central banks. If ever there was a case to be made for the necessity of a large, centralized state institution, this was it. Libertarians forgot that the absence of a central bank and reliance on the gold standard prior to the Federal Reserve Act of 1919 had seen massive periodic financial crises like the one that shook the US in 1908.

Indeed, American neoliberals were hoist, so to speak, with their own petard. From the 1980s onwards the US Treasury Department and institutions like the World Bank and IMF had been advising countries around the world to open up their capital accounts and let investment funds flow freely. They were seeking to undo the capital controls that had been instituted in the wake of the banking crises of the 1930s. From the end of the Second World War up through the 1970s, the global financial system had been highly stable. As liquidity was subsequently encouraged to move unhindered across international borders under the influence of neoliberal ideas, financial crises occurred with alarming regularity. This began with the sterling and Swedish banking crises in the early 1990s, the Mexican peso crisis of 1994, the 1997 Asian financial crisis, and the Russian and Argentine defaults in 1998 and 2001. This process culminated in the 2008 with the US subprime crisis, where global capital had rushed into a poorly regulated American mortgage market and devastated the real economy when it flowed out again.

Neoliberalism had problematic consequences in its support of free trade. The basic doctrine is correct: countries that lower trade barriers with one another will see markets and efficiency expand, leading to higher aggregate incomes for all parties concerned. The rise of East Asia in the late twentieth century and the dramatic fall in global poverty in that period would not have been possible without expanding trade.

Those same trade theorists would, however, have also

explained, *sotto voce*, that not every individual in every country will benefit from free trade. In particular, low-skilled workers in rich countries are likely to lose jobs and opportunities to similarly skilled workers in poor countries as multinational corporations offshore their facilities. The typical answer given to this problem at the time was that workers losing jobs would be compensated through job retraining and other forms of social support. The Clinton Administration bought off trade union opposition to the North American Free Trade Agreement by promising these sorts of programs. But few neoliberal free trade advocates ever expended sufficient time, effort, and resources on these programs as they did on trade facilitation. Many neoliberals supported open immigration, again on the grounds that allowing labor to move to the point of greatest demand would lead to better efficiency. They were again correct in thinking that labor mobility would improve aggregate welfare, but paid less attention to its distributional consequences and the social backlash it would inspire.

In all of these cases there was a political problem: few voters think in terms of aggregate wealth. They don't say to themselves, "Well, I may have lost my job, but at least there's someone else in China or Vietnam, or a new immigrant to my country, who is proportionately much better off." Nor does it make them feel good that the incomes of the owners of the companies that have just laid them off have seen their share prices and bonuses rise, or that they can use their unemployment insurance to buy, at the local Walmart, cheaper consumer goods made in China.

Neoliberals did not just critique state economic intervention; they also criticized social policies that were designed to temper the effects and inequalities produced by market economies. Once again, they began with a correct initial premise: government programs that seek to help people through difficult times frequently create moral hazard. That is, they encourage more of the behavior whose effects they were meant to mitigate. If the state provides generous unemployment insurance, workers might be encouraged to reject jobs they might otherwise take. The US Depression-era program Aid to Families with Dependent Children (AFDC) paid benefits to women raising children on their own. It was meant originally to help women whose husbands were incapacitated or had died, but by the 1980s it was seen as incentivizing poor women to not marry their partners, or to have out-of-wedlock births so as to collect the benefit. There was another set of skewed incentives at work: the administration of social programs had led to the creation of huge bureaucracies in many countries, and those bureaucracies developed an interest in protecting themselves regardless of their performance. In many countries, public sector unions became increasingly powerful, even as their private sector counterparts were losing ground.

This led to a prolonged period in which neoliberal reformers sought to cut back state sectors by ending or scaling back social programs, firing bureaucrats, or seeking to offload programs on to private sector contractors or civil society organizations. In the United States, this effort culminated in the Personal Responsibility and Work Opportunity Reconciliation Act of 1996, which ended AFDC altogether and shifted its funding into block grants to states. Its very title points to the neoliberal premises underlying the legislation. International institutions like the World Bank and the

IMF encouraged similar cutbacks in the developing world under what was called the "Washington Consensus," and in some cases enforced draconian austerity measures on client countries.

The idea of "personal responsibility" is a liberal concept that is built around a true insight, but one that has been carried to extremes by neoliberals. Moral hazard is a reality: if the state pays people not to work, they will work less; if it insures people against too many risks (like building homes in floodplains or in woodland areas of high fire risk), then they will take unwise risks. Underlying many liberal concerns about excessive state intervention was a moral concern that excessive dependency on the state would weaken people's ability to take care of themselves.

But neoliberals and some old-fashioned classical liberals have periodically carried this idea to disastrous extremes. One of the most shameful historical cases was the British decision to continue grain exports during the Irish famine of the late 1840s rather than diverting supplies to feed the Irish population. One-third of Ireland's population died as a result. The reaction of Charles Trevelyan, assistant secretary to the British Treasury, was a case of belief in personal responsibility run amok: he wrote that God had ordained the famine "to teach the Irish a lesson, that calamity must not be too much mitigated . . . The real evil with which we have to contend is not the physical evil of the Famine, but the moral evil of the selfish, perverse and turbulent character of the people."[2]

Liberalism properly understood is compatible with a wide range of social protections provided by the state. Individuals should of course take personal responsibility for their lives and happiness, but there are many circumstances where they face threats that lie well beyond their control. When a person loses a job due to a raging pandemic, temporary government assistance is not fostering dependence, nor is universal access to health care going to make people lazy and improvident. Many people fail to save adequately for their retirements, or do not anticipate unforeseen events that prevent them from working. Forcing people to put aside savings throughout their working careers is not a violation of their fundamental freedoms, but benefits their freedom in the long term.

A basic principle of liberalism should be that individuals are expected to be responsible for their own happiness and life outcomes, but that the state is fully justified in stepping in to support them when they are subject to adverse circumstances beyond their control. The degree of such support depends on the resources and other commitments that the state has. The countries of Scandinavia, with their expansive welfare states, remain liberal societies, much as do the United States or Japan with their relatively smaller state sectors.

Much neoliberal hostility to government is simply irrational. States are necessary to provide public goods that markets by themselves will not provide, from weather forecasting to public health to court systems to food and drug safety to police and national defense. The size of the state is far less important than its quality. In Scandinavia, people often pay more than half their annual incomes in taxes, but in return they get good-quality education up through university, health care, pensions, and other benefits that Americans have to pay for out of their own pockets. By contrast, many poor countries are trapped in a cycle where a poor-quality state fails to provide services, weakening the government's ability to tax and to provide itself with necessary resources. Governments can become bloated, slow, and bureaucratic, and at the same time overly weak and unable to provide necessary services. Liberal states require governments that are strong enough to enforce rules and provide the basic institutional framework within which individuals can prosper.

The result of a generation of neoliberal policies was the world that emerged by the 2010s, in which aggregate incomes were higher than ever, but inequality within countries had also grown enormously.[3] Many countries around the world saw the emergence of a small class of oligarchs, multi-billionaires who could convert their economic resources into political power through lobbyists and purchases of media properties. Globalization enabled them to move their money to low-tax jurisdictions easily, starving states of revenues and making regulation very difficult. Foreign-born populations began to increase in many Western countries, abetted by crises like the Syrian civil war, which sent more than a million refugees into Europe in 2014. All of this paved the way for the populist reaction that became clearly evident in 2016 with Britain's Brexit vote and the election of Donald Trump in the United States.

3

The Selfish Individual

The problems with neoliberal policies were not limited to their immediate economic and political effects; there was a deeper problem with the underlying economic theory itself. This does not make it wrong, but should remind us that it, like all theories, oversimplifies our understanding of human behavior. This means that we need to be careful in the practical conclusions we draw from it, since reality will always be more complex than the theory suggests.

Take the question of property rights, which has been a centerpiece of liberal doctrine from the beginning. Recent interest among economists in property rights was revived at the beginning of the 1980s as a result of the work of writers such as the economic historian Douglass North, who transformed development theory by introducing the factor of institutions—that is, persistent rules that coordinate social activity—as a key explanatory variable for economic growth. (Hard as it is to believe, prior to North most orthodox economic theories of growth failed to take politics, culture, or any other non-economic factors into account.) When North spoke of institutions, he was thinking primarily of property rights and contract enforcement, and an entire generation of development economists subsequently regarded these institutions as the holy grail of growth.[1]

There was of course an important core of truth in the focus on property rights: countries like the former Soviet Union, Cuba, or Venezuela that have engaged in wholesale nationalizations of private property have had huge problems with innovation and growth. No one will invest serious money in a business if they think it will be capriciously taken away by the government. But a singular focus on property rights is neither a magic formula for development nor a path to a just society. As Deirdre McCloskey has shown, North never demonstrated empirically that secure property rights were key to Europe's explosive economic growth after the seventeenth century, as opposed to other factors like the shift towards bourgeois social values that took place at the same time, or the development of the scientific method.[2]

Moreover, strong defense of any existing set of property rights is justified only if the original distribution of property was itself just. Many economists implicitly begin from John Locke's premise that private property arises when human beings settle an uninhabited *terra nullius* and mix their labor with the "worthless things of nature" to create property that is useful to human beings. But what if that property was initially acquired by violence or theft? Agrarian societies were based on giant estates held by aristocrats whose ancestors were warriors who had simply conquered those territories. Their land was worked by peasants who after a bad harvest or sickness would go into debt, and on failure to repay would have their assets seized under rules established by the local lord. This form of property ownership has been a huge obstacle to both economic growth and democracy in contemporary countries from Pakistan to the Philippines. By contrast, Japan, South Korea, and Taiwan under American tutelage engaged in massive land reform in the late 1940s that broke up large estates. This redistribution of property has been widely credited as a basis for their subsequent economic success, not to speak of their ability to turn into successful liberal democracies.

The Lockean story about the origins of private property is also questionable in the United States and other places that were once called lands of "new settlement" like Canada, Australia, New Zealand, Argentina, or Chile. These regions were of course newly settled only by Europeans, being inhabited by a wide variety of indigenous peoples whose ancestors had migrated there perhaps 12,000 years earlier. These people were killed, enslaved, driven off their lands, and swindled, or else died from European diseases. These indigenous groups for the most part did not have anything like European-style property rights with its apparatus of cadastral surveys, land registries, and court systems. Rather, as pastoralists or hunter-gatherers, they enjoyed what would today be described as forage, usufructuary or access rights.

There is no question that European-style property rights made the land far more productive, and this higher level of productivity may have improved the living standards of everyone including those whose lands were appropriated. But the end does not necessarily justify the means. The indigenous peoples lost much more than land; they lost an entire way of life as their land was converted into modern private property.

Another branch of neoliberal economic theory that is intrinsically questionable and has led to some very problematic political consequences had to do with the enthroning of consumer welfare as the ultimate measure of economic well-being, and the implications this choice has had for policy domains like antitrust and trade. This shift was associated intimately with the Chicago School, and figures like Aaron Director, George Stigler, and above all the legal scholar Robert Bork.

Since the passing of the Sherman Antitrust Act in 1890, American policymakers had worried about the impact of giant corporations (or "trusts") on American democracy. Over the subsequent century, the US Justice Department and Federal Trade Commission initiated antitrust suits against large corporations that used their market power to stifle competition. There was in addition a school associated with Justice Louis Brandeis, who believed that the Sherman Act was intended also to serve political goals like the protection of small producers.

The legal scholar and later Solicitor General Robert Bork argued that antitrust law should have one, and only one, goal, which was to maximize consumer welfare, understood either in terms of prices or quality.[3] Bork maintained that the Sherman Act was never intended to serve political aims, and that antitrust law would become incoherent if it did not have a single measurable objective such as the maximization of consumer welfare. He made the case that large corporations often got that way because they were more efficient than smaller ones, and that the government should not stand in the way of their growth. He and his fellow Chicagoans successfully persuaded two generations of economists and legal scholars to adopt the consumer welfare standard as the sole measure of economic outcomes in antitrust cases, which led to a much more relaxed government attitude towards large corporations and mega-mergers.

Bork was correct that the consumer welfare standard provides the legal system with a useful way of resolving a certain class of economic disputes. If Walmart or Amazon, for example, enter a market and threaten the livelihoods of a multitude of small mom-and-pop retailers, how do we judge the demands of the latter that they be protected against competition? The consumer welfare standard would dictate that they would have to give way to the giant retailers because the latter were selling the same goods at much lower prices. Modern economics would dictate that those mom-and-pop retailers close their stores and reinvest their time and capital in another activity that is more productive. The Brandeisians had no clear rule for how to allocate the consumer surplus between consumers and retailers who were locked in a zero-sum struggle.

And yet, many societies can and do protect small producers at the expense of economic efficiency, because they believe that there are social goods other than consumer welfare. This has been done by France and Japan, for example, both of which sought to block the entry of huge American corporations into their markets. Would France be better off if its thousands of cafés were driven out of business by Starbucks, even if the latter offered cheaper or better coffee? Would Japan's quality of life improve if its small sushi bars and tempura restaurants were replaced by large American-style restaurant chains? Indeed, is the United States better off seeing its downtown retailers driven out of business, first by big-box stores like Walmart, and then by online retailers like Amazon? Perhaps this was all technologically inevitable, but one might think that the trade-off between consumer welfare and intangible goods like neighborhoods and ways of living should be open to democratic choice. There may be no economic theory dictating how this choice can be made, but it can be decided through democratic political contestation. There is no reason why economic efficiency needs to trump all other social values.

Consumer welfare is also problematic as a standard of economic well-being, because it fails to capture intangible aspects of well-being. Today's large internet platforms may offer consumers free services, but they gain access to private data in ways that those consumers may not be aware of, and of which they may not approve.

There is a deeper philosophical issue underlying this policy question, which is whether human beings are simply consuming animals whose well-being is measured by how much they consume, or producing animals whose happiness depends on their ability to shape nature and exercise their creative faculties. Contemporary neoliberalism has clearly opted for the former, but there are other traditions that argue that humans are both consuming and producing animals, and that human happiness lies somewhere in a balance between the two. The philosopher Hegel argued that human autonomy rested in work and the ability to transform given nature; that was what in the modern world gave dignity to the slave and made the slave an equal of the master. Karl Marx inherited this idea from Hegel, and said that human beings were both consuming and producing animals.

Communist societies tended to value production over consumption to bad effect: they had "heroes of socialist labor" but no food on the shelves in their stores. The rise of neoliberalism has shifted the pendulum far over to the other side. US workers who had lost their jobs to less expensive labor overseas were told that they nonetheless could buy cheaper goods imported from China. Very few people today would want to shift back to a communist-style emphasis on production over consumption. But would people be willing to sacrifice a bit of consumer welfare in order to maintain the dignity of labor and livelihoods at home? This is a choice that has not been offered to voters under the hegemony of neoliberal ideas.[4]

It may turn out that this is less of a trade-off than we think. The economist Thomas Philippon has argued that American consumer prices are now broadly higher than those in Europe compared to what they were two decades ago, precisely because the United States has failed to enforce its antitrust laws and allowed large corporations to choke off competition.[5] Industrial concentration has other bad effects: large corporations have deep pockets and can fund legions of lobbyists to lock in their existing advantages. This becomes an acute problem for democracy when the main business of those corporations is the news and information that shapes political discourse, and this is one of the reasons that the large internet platforms—Twitter, Facebook, and Google—have come under special scrutiny.[6]

There was another strand of neoliberal thought that took root in the late twentieth century that provided an alternative model of collective action from that of mainstream neoclassical economics, which was the theory of spontaneous order promoted by the Austrian school of Ludwig von Mises and Friedrich Hayek. Hayek in particular observed that the order we see in the natural world was not the result of a divine designer who taught birds to sing or bees to make honey, but rather emerged through the random evolutionary interaction of atoms and molecules that ultimately organized themselves up a chain of beings of increasing complexity, from cells to multicellular organisms to the plants and animals that populate our world. He argued that human social order originated in a similar fashion: individual human agents interacted; the social groups that were more successful replicated themselves not genetically but culturally, while those leading to bad outcomes disappeared. The great example of this was the evolution of markets, where individual buyers and sellers interacted in an unplanned fashion to produce prices signaling relative scarcity, thereby allocating goods more efficiently than central planners ever could. Hayek further argued that English common law was superior to the Continent's civil law in that it evolved from the decisions of countless decentralized judges under the principle of *stare decisis* (precedent), rather than being centrally dictated by legal experts.[7]

Hayek was right about the superior allocative efficiency of markets; he essentially won his famous debate in the 1940s with the other great economist of the period, Joseph Schumpeter, over whether markets or central planning would be the superior economic system. His ideas were taken up by others. When the internet took off in the 1990s, many techno-libertarians became enamored with the idea of spontaneous order, and saw the emerging digital world as one of its wondrous products. Complexity theory, elaborated at places like the Santa Fe Institute, sought to formalize the idea of self-organization and produced genuine insights about how order often originated in a decentralized manner, from flocking birds to indigenous communities agreeing to share resources without the benefit of governments.[8]

But the theory can be carried to extremes. Both Hayek and the techno-libertarians were hostile to the state, which they felt frequently got in the way of human self-organization. But this hostility was driven more by ideology than by empirical observation. As most economists will admit, there are many types of public goods that markets will simply never provide; even if rigid central planning is self-undermining, states have often played helping, coordinating functions, which, for example, promoted economic growth in countries like Japan or South Korea during their high-growth periods. The internet itself was not the product of spontaneous order; its underlying technologies were created as a result of US government investment, often done through the Department of Defense, in things like semiconductors, integrated circuits, and the mandating of network protocols like TCP/IP. Once it was privatized by the US government, the internet did not remain a decentralized network, but rapidly became dominated by two or three gigantic corporations whose power could be challenged only by governments—if they could be challenged successfully at all.

So ideas about the centrality of property rights, consumer welfare, and spontaneous order are far more ambiguous in their economic, political, and moral consequences than neoliberal doctrine would suggest. But there are even deeper problems with modern economics that did not arise with the Chicago School, problems that go back to the fundamental model underlying all of modern neoclassical economics.

Modern economics is built around an assumption that

human beings are "rational utility maximizers," meaning that they use their considerable cognitive skills to maximize their individual self-interest.* There is no question that human beings are typically greedy, individually selfish, and smart, and that they therefore respond to material incentives in the ways that economists suggest. Without individual incentives, centrally planned communist economies were a disaster. When China permitted peasants to keep the earnings from their family plots under the household responsibility system instead of working on collective farms, wheat output went from 55 to 87 million tons in four years.[9]

But key parts of this model are deeply flawed and fly in the face of our day-to-day experience. We will discuss whether human beings are actually rational in a later chapter, and the maximizing part of the theory has been questioned by critics from Herbert Simon to contemporary behavioral economists. But for now I want to focus on another aspect of the model, which is the assumption that human beings act first and foremost as individuals.

Economists build an entire theory of social behavior on top of this individualistic premise. The economic theory of collective action argues that individuals come together in groups primarily as a means of maximizing their own individual interests, and not out of any natural sociability. Again, this assumption yields some important insights. Prior to the publication of Mancur Olson's 1965 book *The*

---

* Some economists try to broaden the utility function to include altruism or other social-regarding behaviors as simply another form of individual preference. This makes the theory tautological, saying in effect that human beings will seek to do whatever it is they seek to do.

Logic of Collective Action, many observers assumed that human beings would naturally collaborate.[10] Olson pointed out that people have incentives to join groups to partake of the benefits the group provides, like national defense or a stable currency. But they also have an incentive to free ride on these benefits, particularly when the size of the group grows and it is hard to monitor the behavior of individual members. This explains behaviors from shirking at work to tax evasion.

Since the publication of Olson's book, a huge amount of game theory has been applied to understand under what conditions individuals would agree to cooperate in groups, some of which has led to genuinely useful insights. There is a large body of economic theory—under the heading of "principal-agent theory"—that makes use of these individualistic premises to explain the behavior of people in large hierarchical organizations. The theory is particularly applicable to narrowly economic behavior, such as firms deciding when to collaborate to fix prices, or how bond traders will react to shifting risk profiles. But in the end it is radically inadequate as a way of understanding the totality of human behavior.

While human beings often act as selfish individuals, they are also intensely social creatures who cannot be individually happy without the support and recognition provided by their peers. In this they are driven not so much by their rationality and material desires as by their emotions. Feelings of pride, anger, guilt, and shame are all related to shared social norms. While the specific content of those norms is culturally determined, the human propensity to follow norms is genetically hardwired into all but the most hardened sociopaths. This is something we can see in the behavior of young children on the playground, who do not have to be taught by their parents to experience shame or embarrassment when they violate the informal norms of their play group. We see the pro-social side of human life in the intense agony and depression felt by isolated people, something made plain to everyone by the recent Covid epidemic that forced everyone to distance themselves from their friends and colleagues.

The human "utility function" therefore includes a lot more than material preferences. Human beings also crave respect, the intersubjective recognition that other humans provide about one's worth or dignity. There is a famous game in experimental economics—the "ultimatum game"—where two players share a pot of money. The first player can divide the pot however he or she wishes; the second player can choose to accept whatever share the first player allocates, or refuse the pot altogether. Running the game repeatedly shows that if the shares are divided roughly equally, the second player almost always accepts the division, but if the remaining pot falls below a certain percentage, the second player will very often walk away from the money because of the inequality of the division. This would be an irrational choice if the players were merely maximizing their individual self-interest, but makes sense if we assume they have feelings of pride or self-respect.

Moreover, human beings crave respect not just for themselves, but also for external things like religious beliefs, social rules, and traditions, even when such craving leads them to behavior that is individually costly. This means that human beings cannot "maximize" in the manner suggested by the basic economic model, which assumes that people have stable preferences. They must trade off incompatible desires in ways that are hard to predict in advance. This is the essence of human autonomy: people constantly make choices between material self-interest and intangible goods like respect, pride, principle, and solidarity, and in ways that cannot be accommodated by the basic utility maximization model. This is particularly true in organizations, where behavior typically conforms to expectations set by peers rather than by any simple calculation of individual self-interest. If human beings were simple maximizing machines, they would never serve in combat or even take the time to vote.

The individualistic premise on which liberal theory is based is therefore not wrong, but rather incomplete. If we take a long historical view, individualism is something that evolved over the centuries, and has become central to modern self-understanding.[11] In earlier stages of human social development—when the dominant forms of organization were bands, segmentary lineages, or tribes—most human beings were tightly bound in fixed social groups and had little opportunity to express individual preferences. This lack of autonomy applied not just to economic choices, but to decisions about where to live, whom to marry, what occupation to take up, or what religious beliefs to profess. The modernization process that has been taking place over the past millennium has slowly liberated people from these social strictures.

Individualism in the family was the mother of all individualisms. In traditional societies, kinship is the dominant structuring principle of social order. It is not governments but relatives who established rules limiting individual choice. As I explained in *The Origins of Political Order*, extended kinship groups began to lose their power first in Europe, where the Catholic Church in early medieval times changed inheritance rules to weaken the ability of kin groups to control the inheritance of property.[12] The Germanic barbarians who overran the Roman Empire had been organized into patrilineal tribes, but their conversion to Christianity quickly dissolved these tribal bonds and replaced them with more contractual and individualistic relationships of dominance and subordination, what we label feudalism. European law began to formally protect the right of individuals, as opposed to kin groups, to buy, sell, and inherit property, extending these rights to women as well as men. This tendency was most pronounced in England, which unsurprisingly became the birth nation of modern individualism.

It is therefore no accident that England was also the birthplace of modern capitalism. Modern markets are dependent on the impersonality of transactions: if you are forced to buy and sell primarily from kinsmen, the economic scale and efficiency you can hope to achieve will be limited. The institutions of property rights and contract enforcement by third parties like courts and arbitrators were designed to widen the scope of markets and permit strangers to interact. The economic growth fostered by economic individualism was therefore one of the great drivers of its spread throughout the world.

It is absurd to think that at this point in history we can reverse course and somehow walk back modern individualism, which would mean walking back the last thousand years of human history. Liberal individualism does not preclude or deny human sociability; it simply means that most social engagements in a liberal society will ideally be voluntary. You can join with other people, but what groups you join are, to the maximum extent possible, a matter of personal choice. This is what creates the civil society we see around us. The core promise of liberalism to protect individual choice remains intensely desired by modern people, not just people in the West where liberalism and individualism were born, but now across the planet in every society that is in the process of modernizing. But because human beings are also inherently social creatures, this expanding individualism has always been received with ambivalence. While individuals have forever resented the strictures placed on them by "society," they have at the same time craved the bonds of community and social solidarity, and felt lonely and alienated in their individualism.

The problem with neoliberalism in economics was thus not that it began from false premises. Its premises were often correct; they were simply incomplete and often historically contingent. The doctrine's defect was to carry those premises to an extreme where property rights and consumer welfare were worshipped, and all aspects of state action and social solidarity denigrated.

4

The Sovereign Self

Individual autonomy was carried to an extreme by liberals on the right who thought primarily about economic freedom. But it was also carried to extremes by liberals on the left, who valued a different type of autonomy centered around individual self-actualization. While neoliberalism threatened liberal democracy by creating excessive inequality and financial instability, liberalism on the left evolved into modern identity politics, versions of which then began to undermine the premises of liberalism itself. The concept of autonomy was absolutized in ways that threatened social cohesion, and in its service progressive activists began to enlist social pressure and the power of the state to silence voices critical of their agenda.

The expansion of the realm of individual autonomy took place in two domains. The first was philosophical, where the meaning of personal autonomy was steadily broadened from choice within an established moral framework, to the ability to choose the framework itself. The second was political, where autonomy came to mean autonomy not for an individual but for the group in which the individual was embedded. The first of these developments absolutized autonomy over all other human goods, while the second ended up disputing some of the underlying premises of liberalism itself, like the latter's stress on human universalism or its requirement of tolerance.

Autonomy, or choice, has for long been understood in Western thought to be the characteristic that makes human beings human, and is thereby the basis for human dignity. This begins with the story of Adam and Eve in the book of Genesis: Adam and Eve disobey God's command and eat from the Tree of the Knowledge of Good and Evil, and are thereby cast out of the Garden of Eden. They make the wrong choice, and this original sin burdens mankind henceforth with pain, toil, and labors. But it also endows them with the capacity for moral choice, which they did not have in their original state of innocence. This capacity for choice gives human beings an intermediate moral status. They are higher than the rest of created nature, because they, unlike animals or plants, can make choices and are not merely driven by their natures; but they are lower than God because they can choose wrongly. One might add that in the Bible story, their capacity for choice does not extend to making the moral law itself, but simply to obeying it; only God has that ability to determine the nature of right and wrong.

The story in Genesis contains a very deep insight about human nature. We see the transition from innocence to a knowledge of good and evil in the development of every human child. No one blames an infant for crying or wetting their diapers; children are born, in a sense, without moral knowledge and they act on instinct. But as they develop from young children into adults, they are exposed to ideas of right and wrong, and their moral sense develops in a way that allows them to make choices. Different cultures and legal systems around the world set differing ages for the transition to adulthood, but no culture fails to hold adults responsible for obeying its rules. We know that individual choice is highly conditioned by the environment that a child grows up in—family, friends, socioeconomic status, and the like—as well as by genetic factors over which an individual has no control. Many legal systems see these exogenous factors as mitigating circumstances that affect how a society deals with a rule-breaker. But no society today or historically has said that its members are thereby broadly exonerated from any form of personal accountability, and every legal system in the world is based on the notion that there is some reservoir of individual choice that makes people accountable for their actions.

This original Judeo-Christian insight was further developed by Martin Luther, and became the doctrinal basis for the Protestant Reformation. According to Luther, the essence of Christianity was faith alone, an inner state that may not be accessible even to the believer. It did not reside in an individual's conformity with the rituals and rules set by the Catholic Church. This laid the foundation for subsequent ideas about the existence of an occluded inner self that was distinct from the outer self visible to the rest of society.

The idea of an inner self is not unique to Western Christianity. Hinduism, for example, is built around the idea of an inner soul that can migrate over time and across different physical bodies. But most societies historically have prized conformity with their established external rules over expression of the desires of that inner self. What Luther did was to change the valence of inner and outer: the entire institutional structure of the Catholic Church could be wrong, and an individual believer with faith right. Protestantism was built around individual believers reading the Bible who could come to their own conclusions about the Word of God. This set off a revolution against the Church, and plunged Europe into a century and a half of religious warfare over the locus of Christian belief.

Luther's valorization of the inner self did not thereby liberate the self to choose whatever it wanted. Luther remained within a Christian framework: human beings had the power of choice, but it was a power to have faith in God's Word or not. In subsequent centuries, Enlightenment thinkers began to question the authority not just of the Church, but of religion as such. The act of choice came to be seen as something separate from and more valuable than the substance of what was being chosen. By the time of the French Revolution, Luther's Christian freedom had evolved into the Rights of Man. These rights were connected with choice, but de-linked from the religious framework in which it had been embedded.

The valorization of inner over outer was given a secular form, most notably in the work of Jean-Jacques Rousseau, who argued that all human evil began when happy, isolated individuals in the state of nature came together in society. Rousseau reversed the Bible story, which found Adam and Eve guilty of an original sin that needed to be expiated. He argued that human beings were naturally good, and became bad only when they entered into society and started comparing themselves to one another. But he argued that humans were also "perfectible," meaning that they were undetermined by what we would now call their cultural environments, and could choose to recover their natural goodness. He posited an idea that became foundational in modern thought, that we have deeply hidden inner natures that are smothered by the layers of social rules imposed on us by the society surrounding us. Autonomy for him meant recovery of that authentic inner self, and escape from the social rules that imprisoned it.

The other Enlightenment thinker who was critical to the self-understanding of modern liberalism was Immanuel Kant. Kant picked up on Rousseau's idea of perfectibility, and turned it into the core of his moral philosophy. At the beginning of the *Foundations of the Metaphysics of Morals*, he says that the only thing that is unconditionally good is a good will, and that the capacity to make moral choices is what makes us distinctively human. Human beings are ends in themselves and should never be treated as a means to other ends. In this we can see a secular echo of the Christian idea of man, made in the image of God, based on his or her capacity for moral choice. But unlike Christian freedom, Kantian morality is rooted in abstract rules of reason rather than the revealed Word of God. It lays the basis for liberal universalism and equality: people of different nationalities have an equal capacity for moral choice. As in the case of the Universal Church, this equal dignity means that all people must be treated with equal respect, a respect that would be formalized through a system of law.

Kant prioritized the act of choice itself over any of the particular ends or "goods" that human beings seek. He did not root this priority in empirical observations about the nature of political conflict. Rather, this priority came directly out of his metaphysics. Kant distinguished between the phenomenal and noumenal realms. The former was the world as presented to us by ordinary experience, a chaotic jumble of sensations, memories, and perceptions, organized by the human subject through the manifolds of time and space. The second realm was the kingdom of ends, the domain in which individual "choosing subjects" were situated, and one that was not governed by the deterministic laws of physics. That choosing subject was prior to its specific attributes, such as family, social status, and possessions. The moral rules that Kant derived, like the rule that people should be treated as ends in themselves and never as a means to an end, were rules of reason that flowed from his a priori assumptions, and not from any form of empirical observation. This approach to moral reasoning is sometimes labeled "deontological" because it is not linked to any ontology or substantive theory of human nature that specifies the ends that human beings actually pursue.

The Anglo-American approach to liberal theory was anything but deontological. Thomas Hobbes begins *Leviathan* with an explicit theory of human nature, providing a catalog of human passions that places the fear of violent death at the summit of the human "bads" that his social contract seeks to mitigate. Hobbes's account of the "state of nature" is actually a metaphor for a theory of human nature; while his differs from the one given by John Locke in the *Second Treatise on Government*, they both base their theories on explicit accounts of the hierarchy of substantive ends pursued by human beings. Their theories of natural right were carried forward by Thomas Jefferson, who based his claims for American independence on the "self-evident" proposition that "all men are created equal."

Today, hardly any theorist professes to believe in the natural right arguments of Hobbes, Locke, or Jefferson. Over time in liberal societies, there has been a growing reluctance to posit substantive human ends that have priority over other ends; rather, it is the act of choice itself that has the highest priority. The Anglo-American tradition of liberalism converges with the Continental approach of Immanuel Kant in the person of John Rawls, the Harvard professor whose *Theory of Justice* has become the dominant articulation of contemporary liberal theory.[1]

Rawls like Kant sought to derive rules for a liberal society that were not based on a substantive theory of human nature or empirical observation of the ends that human beings actually seek. He argued, similarly to Kant, that justice is prior to the good—that is, that rules protecting choice of goods have priority over any particular good that individuals seek. Rawls did not want, however, to rely on Kant's metaphysics and its postulate of a noumenal realm separate from the phenomenal world. His device to get to these abstract rules lay in his concept of the "original position," that is, a situation in which individuals could agree on fair rules for their society, once they were stripped of any knowledge of the actual position they held in that society. Behind this "veil of ignorance," Rawls argued, no one would choose a rule that disadvantaged the weakest members of society, since they would not know in advance if they would be in that group. He went on to argue that the human subject is separate from its attributes, such as property, wealth, social status, character, or indeed genetic endowment, all of which are contingent facts distributed in arbitrary ways. This lays the groundwork for his justification of an extensive welfare state in a liberal society. He argued that contingent attributes like property or even natural ability were the common property of the society as a whole, and could be redistributed to serve the interests of the least well-off.

Rawlsian liberalism has become the center of contemporary discussions of liberal theory and remains the dominant self-understanding of many liberals, particularly in the academic and legal communities. There is a parallel between the shift from economic liberalism to neoliberalism, and the evolution of Lockean-Jeffersonian liberalism to the Rawlsian version. In both cases, a strong underlying idea (the benefits of free markets in one case, the value of individual autonomy in the other) was stretched to an unsustainable extreme. In the case of Rawls, the problem lies in the absolutization of autonomy, and the elevation of choice over all other human goods. This absolutization is both theoretically objectionable, and has played itself out in problematic ways in liberal societies.

Since the original publication of *A Theory of Justice* in 1971, there have been any number of critiques of Rawls,[2] the most prominent of which have been attacks by libertarian thinkers like Robert Nozick who dispute Rawls's assertion that individuals do not in some sense "own" either their physical possessions or their native abilities.[3] However, there is another significant body of criticism that comes from so-called "communitarian" thinkers like Alasdair MacIntyre, Charles Taylor, Michael Walzer, and Michael Sandel, who dispute the absolute priority that Rawls gives to the choosing self, and to justice over the good.[4]

Michael Sandel describes Rawlsian liberalism as a liberating project that ultimately empties us of meaning:

The deontological universe and the independent self that moves within it, taken together, hold out a liberating vision. Freed from the dictates of nature and the sanction of social roles, the deontological subject is installed as sovereign, cast as the author of the only moral meanings there are . . . as independent selves, we are free to choose our purposes and ends unconstrained . . . by custom or tradition or inherited status. So long as they are not unjust, our conceptions of the good carry weight, whatever they are, simply in virtue of our having chosen them.[5]

But an autonomous self that has been detached from all prior loyalties and commitments "is not to conceive of an ideally free and rational agent, but to imagine a person wholly without character, without moral depth":

Those who dispute the priority of the right argue that justice is relative to the good, not independent of it. As a philosophical matter, our reflections about justice cannot reasonably be detached from our reflections about the nature of the good life and the highest human ends. As a political matter, our deliberations about justice and rights cannot proceed without reference to the conceptions of the good that find expression in the many cultures and traditions within which those deliberations take place.[6]

We can illustrate these rather abstract arguments with a simple example. Compare two individuals in a modern liberal society. One of them spends his time playing video games, surfing the web, and living off subsidies he gets from his well-off family. He barely graduated from high school, not because he lacked resources or suffered a disability, but simply because he didn't like studying. He likes to smoke weed (which has just been legalized in his state), has no interest in reading about current affairs (or reading more generally), and loves to spend time shopping for products online, when he is not scanning Facebook or leaving snarky comments on Instagram. Beyond connecting on social media, he is not particularly involved with or supportive of his circle of friends; when asked to help out victims of a traffic accident he witnessed, he walked away.

The second individual graduated from high school and went on to community college, having to work while studying because her mother, raising her as a single parent, could not afford college tuition. She pays attention to public affairs, and reads as many newspapers and books as she can spare the time for. She hopes eventually to complete a four-year university degree and ultimately become a lawyer or go into public service. As a person, she is generous and has many deep friendships with a broad variety of people, and she has taken risks in her life in advocating for people she believes were wrongfully accused. Neither she nor the first individual act in ways that prevent other people around them from making comparable choices.

John Rawls's theory of justice would not allow either public authorities or the rest of us to pass judgment on these two individuals, and say that we found the woman to be morally superior to the man in any way. Both are following life plans that they have set for themselves. Rawls would argue that these plans are heavily influenced by contingent social factors like the family and neighborhood each grew up in, as well as by the genetic endowments given them by their parents. In that sense, they are not completely autonomous agents, but heavily influenced by their contingent characteristics, which for him would explain their differing choices. But unless these individuals seek to prevent other people from acting autonomously, there is no higher ground on which any of us can make judgments of their relative merits. Whereas Lockean liberalism enjoined tolerance for different conceptions of the good, Rawlsian liberalism enjoins non-judgmentalism regarding other people's life choices. Indeed, it tends to celebrate difference and diversity per se as liberations from oppressive social constraints.

Had the two individuals in my example differed in terms of race, national origin, or religious heritage, then Rawls would be correct that a liberal state could not discriminate between them since these are characteristics over which they had no control. But where they differ is with regard to their character: the degree to which they are public-spirited, generous, thoughtful, meaningfully connected to the people around them, courageous, well-informed, and interested in improving themselves through education. Character is something that can be deliberately cultivated by individuals, an important part of their autonomy. Exercise of these virtues would appear to be important requirements of a liberal republic. Indeed, there is a tradition described by J. G. A. Pocock, which began with Machiavelli's *Discourses* and crossed the Atlantic to influence the thought of some of the American Founders, that a well-constituted republic had to be built around public-spirited citizens, and would survive or fall based on the content of their characters.[7]

Rawls would argue that one's character—for example whether one was public-spirited or narrowly selfish—was not intrinsic to the autonomous inner self, but a contingent attribute determined by one's cultural or genetic inheritance, no different from skin color or religious upbringing. He, like Kant, would argue that the desire to be educated, or to live in a society with other educated people, was a vision of the good that had no particular priority over other visions or the requirements of justice. (Kant, in fact, has been blamed for inconsistency on this issue, since he elsewhere argues in favor of an educated citizenry.[8])

Rawlsian liberalism provided a philosophical justification for the liberation of the inner self that was occurring concurrently in the broader society, and for an ever-expanding understanding of the scope of personal autonomy. The 1950s probably represented the high point of social consensus and conformity in both the US and Europe. In America, the Republican Party had come to accept the New Deal and welfare state, and overlapped substantially in its policy views with the Democratic Party. In Europe, there was general agreement about the need for a strong welfare state, which was built in Germany and France with substantial input from center-right Christian Democratic parties. Religious affiliation with mainline Protestant and Catholic churches was high in the United States, with 50 percent of Americans reporting that they attended church on a regular basis.[9]

Under this veneer of social conformity, however, new intellectual currents were forming. Personal goals were increasingly set not by institutionalized religion, but by the need for "self-actualization." The elevation of self-actualization could be seen as a contemporary manifestation of Rousseau's inner self, the authentic being that was being smothered and suppressed by social regulation. The social psychologist Abraham Maslow put self-actualization at the apex of human needs, above more pedestrian concerns like family or social solidarity.[10] In doing so, he was supported by a new and rapidly growing infrastructure of therapeutic psychologists, who had increasingly displaced the pastor or parish priest as the source of social solace for people who were troubled or alienated.

The beat generation of the 1950s and the counterculture that emerged during the 1960s took aim at conformity itself as the chief evil preventing the actualization of human potential. The revolt extended to politics, where a New Left appeared to challenge the meliorative politics of mainstream American liberals, whose policies had entangled the country in the Vietnam War. A similar radicalization of politics took place in Europe, with the events of 1968 leading, for example, to the toppling of the iconic Charles de Gaulle as president of France.

In the United States, there was a rapid political backlash against the social turmoil of the 1960s, which led to Richard Nixon's landslide victory in 1968 and his re-election in 1972. The Vietnam debacle and the Watergate scandal deepened the cynicism of many Americans and Europeans about their own institutions, but did not prevent the rise of a new generation of conservative leaders—Ronald Reagan and Margaret Thatcher—in the 1980s. Over the next generation, college campuses calmed down and students appeared more focused on job security and career advancement than on social issues or politics.

Reaganism's main policy thrust was focused on a different

version of liberal autonomy, the neoliberal agenda of removing the state from the regulation of private markets and the maximization of economic freedom. Nonetheless, by relentlessly attacking the state and the idea of collective action, Reaganism served to delegitimize existing institutions and increase cynicism about the potential role of government. Though Reagan remained personally popular throughout his presidency, generalized social distrust began its relentless climb upward in this period.[11]

The veneer of social and political conservatism masked massive changes that were taking place under the surface. The desire for self-actualization did not disappear; it was simply diverted from politics and overt countercultural activism into something more deeply personal. Tara Isabella Burton describes this transformation as "remixed religion," where conformity with institutional religion was replaced by "intuitional" religion that could be assembled from any number of pieces as a matter of individual choice.[12] Many Americans supplemented or simply replaced Christianity with a variety of Eastern religions like Hinduism or Buddhism, which provided them with a pathway to spirituality that seemed blocked by mainline churches. Millions of other people began to practice watered-down versions of Hinduism in the form of yoga and meditation, which directly focused attention on the recovery of the inner self. They believed they were doing this in search of exercise or mental health, while unconsciously buying into the idea that recovery of their deeply hidden self would be their ultimate source of happiness.

There were other dimensions to this search for the inner self, such as the "wellness" and "self-care" movements, and the emphasis on personal health through practices like eating organic foods. People of course need to care for their bodies, but "wellness" took on a spiritual meaning for many Americans, actively promoted by corporations seeking to make money by convincing consumers that their products would enhance not just the body but the soul as well. One example Burton gives is SoulCycle, the exercise studio that provided not just aerobic training, but, according to its promotional materials, a path to being a better person ("a Renegade, a Hero, a Warrior"), as well as the sense of community that traditional religion had once provided. Other manifestations of the ongoing search for the inner self are mindfulness courses, meditation apps, and self-care products in which health products, organic foods, and skin creams are marketed as means of recovering and protecting the "authentic you." If therapists had begun to displace ministers and priests in the 1950s and 1960s as healers of spiritual distress, the 2000s saw the rise of internet "influencers" displace therapists as people to go to for help.

The self-care and wellness movements are simply contemporary manifestations of Rousseau's vision of the "plenitude" of the inner self. That self is good, and its recovery is the original fount of human happiness. But it has been polluted by an outer society that feeds us unhealthy foods full of pesticides and artificial flavors, that sets goals and expectations that build anxiety and self-doubt, and by competitive urges that undermine our self-esteem. Instead of worshipping God, we need to worship ourselves, a self that is hidden by doubts and uncertainty, just as God was once hidden from Martin Luther. Rather than seeking the false esteem of others, we need to esteem ourselves. This is what ultimately gives us agency and control over our lives.

Rawlsian liberalism started out as a project to defend individual choice from oppressive social control. Rawls explicitly targeted utilitarian versions of liberalism articulated by thinkers like Jeremy Bentham who argued that the good of the greater number could override the rights of individuals. Rawls's defense of justice over the good was rooted in a desire to protect dissident individuals from established opinion, such as those promoted by traditional religions. While very few people in contemporary liberal societies have read Rawls, his views have filtered down into the popular culture in many ways, and into the American legal system. We believe we have inner selves whose freedom is being restricted by a host of existing institutions, from family to workplaces to political authorities. In many quarters, dissidence is celebrated, and it is being judgmental that is condemned. Freedom to choose extends not just to the freedom to act within established moral frameworks, but to choose the framework itself.

One might ask, what is so terrible about a society in which individuals seek to actualize themselves in diverse ways, from yoga to health diets to Soul Cycling, as long as they don't violate Rawls's principle of justice and prevent other individuals from actualizing themselves? In what way is this a threat to liberalism, rather than being an implementation of liberal ideas?

There are two answers to this question. The first is that belief in the sovereignty of the individual deepens liberalism's tendency to weaken other forms of communal engagement, and in particular turns people away from virtues like public-spiritedness that are needed to sustain a liberal polity overall. It keeps people locked into what Tocqueville observed were the "little communities" of family and friends, rather than engagement with politics more broadly.

The second problem is the opposite of the first. Many people will never be content with the individual sovereignty they are told they are free to exercise. They will recognize that their inner selves are not sovereign, as Rawls suggests, but heavily shaped by external forces like racism and patriarchy. Autonomy needs to be exercised not so much by individuals, as by the groups of which they are members. Rawls's assertion that rational individuals will assent to the principles of the original position overestimates human rationality, and would seem to be empirically wrong.[13] The type of liberalism that seeks to be relentlessly neutral with regard to "values" eventually turns on itself by questioning the value of liberalism itself, and becomes something that is not liberal.

5

Liberalism Turns on Itself

As explained in my book *Identity*, the idea that each of us has an authentic inner self that demands respect and recognition has been around for a long time in Western thought. Such identities are diverse, multiple, and omnipresent. On the other hand, "identity politics" tends to focus on a fixed characteristic like race, ethnicity, or gender. These characteristics are seen not just as one of many belonging to an individual, but rather an essential component of the inner self, one that demands social recognition.

There are many parts of the world in which identity politics is very pronounced. The Balkans, Afghanistan, Myanmar, Kenya, Nigeria, India, Sri Lanka, Iraq, Lebanon, and other countries are divided into clearly demarcated ethnic or religious groups, and loyalty to those smaller identities often takes precedence over larger national identities. Identity politics makes liberalism difficult to implement in such societies; I will discuss the political strategies used to reconcile demands for group recognition in chapter 9.

In the United States, identity politics got its start on the left, where marginalized groups such as African Americans, women, gay people, and others began to demand equal recognition in a series of social movements beginning in the

1960s.* Identity politics was a powerful mobilizational tool that could help advance the rights of these communities. It was a means of helping individuals to understand the ways in which they had suffered injustice and unequal treatment, and what they had in common with other members of their group.

Identity politics initially emerged as an effort to fulfill the promise of liberalism, which preached a doctrine of universal equality and equal protection of human dignity under the law. Actual liberal societies, however, failed to live up to those ideals in grievous ways. After the Civil War and passage of the Thirteenth, Fourteenth, and Fifteenth Amendments, segregation and highly unequal opportunities for African Americans were deeply entrenched in many parts of the United States. Women did not have the right to vote until the 1920s in most liberal democracies, and were largely excluded from the workplace until the 1960s. Homosexuality was criminalized in most democracies, and gay men and lesbians remained socially closeted for even longer. Internationally, the colonial domination of much of the world continued until well after the Second World War, led by leading liberal powers like Britain and France.

Women have had to endure a spectrum of wrongs from

---

*White identity politics has long existed; the Ku Klux Klan was founded by defeated Confederates like Nathan Bedford Forrest who believed that the South had been unjustly conquered in the "war of Northern aggression," and that whites needed to assert the supremacy of their race in its aftermath. Outside the South and its borderlands, however, most white Americans did not see themselves first and foremost as victimized white people, but as Americans who happened to be white.

time immemorial, from sexual harassment up through rape and other forms of violence, a situation made critical by their massive entry into labor markets beginning in the 1960s. These wrongs were endured on an individual basis for the most part until the rise of the #MeToo movement, which, as the hashtag indicated, revealed harassment to be a common experience shared by a broad category of women. It was this shifting consciousness of shared experience that powered a political movement to change laws and norms regarding the interaction of women and men. Similarly, African Americans have been, and continue to be, disproportionately the victims of arrest and incarceration, have received longer sentences for equivalent crimes, and have long been subject to daily indignities like police stops and searches in ways that white people have not. In a democratic political system, the only way such unequal treatment can be remedied is through political action: citizens, both black and white, have to understand the nature of racism, and be mobilized to demand political action to combat it.

Understood in this fashion, identity politics seeks to complete the liberal project, and achieve what was hoped to be a "color-blind" society. It was under this banner that the Civil Rights movement of the 1960s ended legal segregation and brought about major legal changes like the Civil Rights and Voting Rights Acts. Activists began challenging discriminatory laws throughout the South, brutal police and vigilante responses enflamed public opinion, and the movement grew in size. The goals of movement leaders like Martin Luther King were simply to have African Americans fully included in the broader national identity as promised by the Fourteenth Amendment.

As time went on, however, the critique began to shift from liberalism's failure to live up to its own ideals, to a critique of liberal ideas in themselves and the doctrine's underlying premises. This critique targeted its emphasis on individualism, its claims of moral universality, and its relationship to capitalism.

In recent years, there has been a noisy fight in the United States over "critical race theory" and other critical theories related to ethnicity, gender, gender preference, and other issues. Contemporary avatars of critical theory are more popularizers and political advocates than they are serious intellectuals making sustained arguments, and their right-wing critics (the vast majority of whom have not read a word of critical theory) are even worse. Critical theory made a serious and sustained critique of liberalism's underlying principles, and it is important to go back to the theory's origins. The more extreme versions of critical theory shifted from a critique of liberal practice to a critique of liberalism's underlying essence, and sought to replace it with an alternative illiberal ideology. Once again, we see liberal ideas being stretched to the point of breaking.

One of the precursors of critical theory was Herbert Marcuse. His 1964 book *One-Dimensional Man* and his essay "Repressive Tolerance" served as a road map for later critical theory. Marcuse argued that liberal societies weren't in fact liberal and did not protect either equality or autonomy. Rather, they were controlled by capitalist elites who created a consumer culture that lulled ordinary people into compliance with its rules. Liberty was a mirage that would only be overcome by creating a radically different society:

> And the problem of making possible such a harmony
> between every individual liberty and the other is not
> that of finding a compromise between competitors, or
> between freedom and law, between general and indi-
> vidual interest, common and private welfare in an *estab-
> lished* society, but of *creating* the society in which man
> is no longer enslaved by institutions which vitiate self-
> determination from the beginning.[1]

Similarly, freedom of speech was not an absolute right; the
wrong kind of speech should not be tolerated when exercised by repressive forces defending the status quo.[2]

Marcuse argued, as did many New Left radicals of the
period, that the traditional working class had ceased being
a potentially revolutionary force and had instead become
counterrevolutionary—they had been bought off by capitalism, in effect. He would go on to write about sexuality as a
factor in the struggle for human liberation.[3] Marcuse was
therefore a critical bridge at the juncture between twentieth-
and twenty-first-century progressivism that increasingly
defined inequality not in terms of broad social classes like
bourgeoisie and proletariat, but in terms of narrower identity groups based on race, ethnicity, gender, and sexual
orientation.

The systematic critique of liberalism's underlying principles had several distinct components. It began with a
rejection of the doctrine's premise of primordial individualism. Like Marcuse, progressive critics argued that in existing
liberal societies, individuals were not actually capable of
exercising individual choice. Liberal theorists like Hobbes,
Locke, and Rousseau, or Rawls in his "original position,"

posited isolated individuals in a state of nature who voluntarily chose to enter into a social contract that created civil society. In the words of John Christman,

> Notoriously, Western political philosophy in the modern age—dominated by what is broadly characterized as liberal theory—has assumed that the model of personhood to be utilized in these contexts is fundamentally *individualistic* . . . In addition, the picture of the citizen of the just polity includes no specific reference to the marks of social identity, such as race, gender, sexuality, culture, and so on, that many actual individuals might immediately mention when describing themselves. The model person, in the liberal tradition, is characterized without essential connections with past or present others or social factors external to "him."[4]

Early critical theorists like Charles W. Mills castigated Rawls for writing a theory of justice that failed to deal specifically with one of the biggest historical sources of injustice, the domination of one race by another.[5] This was a feature and not a bug of Rawls's methodology, of course, since his original position requires stripping individuals of all "contingent" characteristics. But the thinness of the remaining autonomous subject was a grave weakness of the theory. Mills in this regard constituted a subset of the "communitarian" critics of Rawls, arguing that there was no choosing individual prior to that individual's specific attributes such as race, gender, or sexual orientation.

Liberalism's critics have further asserted that individualism is a Western concept that does not accord with the more communal traditions of other cultures. Individualism, it has been asserted, never took root in East or South Asia, the Middle East, or sub-Saharan Africa the way it did in Europe and North America; the liberal belief in the universalism of individual human rights thus betrayed a blinkered Eurocentrism.

Flowing from this critique of primordial individualism, critical theorists went on to cite liberalism's failure to recognize the significance of groups. Liberal theory tended to assume that individuals would organize themselves into groups, whether families, companies, political parties, churches, or civil society organizations, all on a voluntary basis. The theory, critics argued, did not take into account the fact that real world societies are organized into involuntary groups in which people are categorized according to characteristics like race or gender over which they have no control. In the words of Ann Cudd,

> We are individuals who belong to social groups, some of which we choose to belong to and some of which we belong to whether or not we would choose to belong if we could. Yet social scientists, philosophers, and theorists have often clouded this picture of social life by ignoring, reducing, or denying one or both kinds of social groups.[6]

The liberal tendency to believe that all group memberships are voluntary is directly embedded in the collective action theories espoused by neoclassical economists; as noted in chapter 3, groups exist only to further the interests of their individual members. Critical theory by contrast argued that the most important groups were the products of dominance of some groups over others.

Flowing from this observation was the related charge that liberalism failed to grant sufficient autonomy to cultural groups, and sought to impose a culture rooted in European values on diverse populations with other traditions. Groups are defined not simply by their victimization, but by the deep cultural traditions that bind them together. Liberal pluralism should thus recognize not only the autonomy of individuals, but the autonomy of the cultural groups that comprise any given society. Cultural autonomy lies in a group's ability to control education, language, customs, and the narratives that define how a particular group understands its origins and present identity.

A third critique of liberalism had to do with its use of contract theory. Hobbes, Locke, Rousseau, and Rawls all explicitly refer to a social contract by which a just society can be formed through voluntary agreement among its members. There are of course variations between them: Hobbes believes that individuals can voluntarily submit to a monarchy, while Locke believes that the contract must be endorsed by explicit consent of the governed. But all assume that parties to the contract are individuals capable of exercising choice.

In *The Sexual Contract*, the feminist writer Carole Pateman attacked the voluntarist assumptions of classical liberal theory. She noted that many early contract theorists believed in the legitimacy of a slave contract: if a weak individual faced a choice between a life of slavery or death at the hands of a stronger person, the former could voluntarily choose to be a slave. Pateman's argument echoed the Marxist critique of the concept of "free labor" in capitalist societies: contracts made between individuals of very different levels of power were not fair simply because they were seemingly voluntary. She noted that this applied particularly to sexual relationships. John Locke, in his *Treatises on Government*, has been traditionally credited with attacking the patriarchal theory of Robert Filmer, which explicitly grounded monarchical authority in the authority of the father over his family. But, Pateman argued, Locke separated political society from the natural society of the family; the former was voluntary and consensual, while the latter remained natural and hierarchical. She argued that the new political society thus formed liberated only the sons:

> Sex-right or conjugal right, the original political right, then becomes completely hidden. The concealment was so beautifully executed that contemporary political theorists and activists can "forget" that the private sphere also contains—and has its genesis in—a contractual relationship between two adults. They have found nothing surprising in the fact that, in modern patriarchy, women, unlike sons, never emerge from their "nonage" and the "protection" of men; we never interact in civil society on the same basis as men.[7]

Women were excluded from the contract, and could not be incorporated into civil society because they "naturally lack the capacities required to become civil individuals."[8]

Charles Mills went on to extend this critique of contract theory to race as well as gender. The US Constitution was an explicit contract establishing the new country, but it was based on the exclusion of African Americans from citizenship and overtly counted them as three-fifths of a person for apportionment purposes. Mills argued that, as in the case of the sexual contract, this exclusion was hidden from view amid the celebratory reverence that the white citizens of the United States expressed for their own origins.[9]

A fourth critique of liberalism argued that the doctrine could not be dissociated from the most rapacious forms of capitalism, and therefore would continue to produce exploitation and gross inequalities. In chapters 2 and 3 above, I argued that "neoliberalism" was a particular interpretation of economic liberalism that prevailed in the United States and other countries at a particular historical moment. Samuel Moyn among others argues that this connection was not contingent but inevitable: liberalism with its emphasis on individualism and property rights inevitably leads to neoliberalism.[10]

Critical theorists attacked liberalism for its close association with colonialism and for Europe's domination of non-white peoples. Postcolonial theory as articulated by writers like Frantz Fanon attacked Western attitudes of cultural superiority that devalued non-Western peoples and their perspectives.[11] It also linked colonialism to capitalism. The Portuguese and then the British established a system of triangular trade across the North Atlantic in the sixteenth and seventeenth centuries in which sugar, rum, and later cotton were exchanged for manufactured goods and slaves. The cotton that served as a critical input making possible the British Industrial Revolution was picked by black slaves in the American South.[12] Pankaj Mishra has written about how liberalism came to have a bad odor in colonized countries such as India or Algeria, where leading liberals like John Stuart Mill or Alexis de Tocqueville were supporters of European domination of other peoples. According to Mishra, Western liberals believed in the universality of liberal values and the underlying model of humans as autonomous individuals only because they were unaware of the very different cultural traditions and assumptions of the territories they had conquered.[13]

A final critique of liberalism is more procedural than substantive. Because liberal societies limit power through constitutional checks and balances, it is very difficult to change policies or institutions. They rely on deliberation and persuasion to bring about change, but these are at best slow vehicles and at worst permanent obstacles to correcting existing injustices. A just society would require a huge and ongoing redistribution of wealth and power, which would be fiercely resisted by their current holders. Political power must thus be exercised at the expense of those check-and-balance institutions.

A great deal of critical theory thus goes well beyond accusing liberalism of hypocrisy and a failure to live up to its own principles, to a condemnation of the doctrine in its essence. Different branches of critical theory make use of variants of Marcuse's argument that ostensibly liberal regimes are in fact not liberal at all but reflect the interests of hidden power structures that dominate and benefit from the status quo. Liberalism's association with different dominant elites, whether capitalists, men, white, or straight people, is not a contingent fact of history; rather, domination is essential to the nature of liberalism and the reason why these different groups support liberalism as an ideology.

These criticisms all fail to hit their target, however, and amount to a charge of guilt by association. Each of the above critiques of liberalism fails to show how the doctrine is wrong in essence. Take the charge that liberalism is too individualistic, and that liberalism is a historically contingent characteristic of European societies. In chapter 3 I explained how this charge can be justly leveled against contemporary neoclassical economic theory, which asserts the primacy of individual self-interest as a universal human characteristic. But the fact that human beings have pro-social as well as selfishly individualistic sides to their personalities can be easily accommodated in a broader understanding of liberalism.

Human sociability takes a huge variety of forms, virtually all of which are permitted to flourish in actual liberal societies. Private associational life has grown enormously as societies become richer and can devote more of their surplus to socially oriented activities. Modern liberal states have dense networks of voluntary civil society organizations that provide community, social services, and advocacy to their members and to the political community more broadly. Nor has liberalism prevented the growth of the state as a locus of community. Welfare states and social protections have grown hugely from the late nineteenth century on, to the point that they consume nearly half of GDP in many advanced liberal democracies.

Individualism did indeed have historical roots in certain parts of Europe, roots that predated the emergence of modern liberalism by nearly a millennium. As noted in chapter 3, it followed on a series of rules introduced by the Catholic Church prohibiting divorce, concubinage, adoption, and cousin marriages, which made it much more difficult for extended kin networks to retain property across generations.

But individualism is hardly a "white" or European characteristic. One of the enduring challenges of human societies is the need to move beyond kinship as a source of social organization, towards more impersonal forms of social interaction. Many non-European societies have employed a range of strategies for reducing the power of kin groups, such as the use of eunuchs in China and the Byzantine Empire, or the Mamluk-Ottoman practice of educating captured slaves, who were chosen on the basis of ability and forbidden to raise families of their own, as soldiers and administrators. Meritocracy was simply another effective strategy for avoiding the need to hire your cousin or child for a job for which they were manifestly unqualified, and choosing the individual most suited to accomplish the task at hand.

Some contemporary proponents of cultural autonomy suggest that quantitative and qualitative reasoning skills measured in practice by standardized examinations are culturally biased against racial minorities. The fact that some racial and ethnic groups do better than others in the aggregate in various activities indicates that culture is indeed an important determinant of outcomes. But the solution to this problem should lie in remediation of those cultural obstacles to success, rather than in devaluing the criterion of success itself.

The view that meritocracy is somehow associated with white identity or Eurocentrism reflects the parochialism of contemporary identity politics. Meritocracy and standardized examinations have clear roots in other non-Western cultures. Examinations were adopted in China because rulers under the pressure of intense military competition found they could not recruit competent lieutenants and administrators without them. They were used in the state of Qin before the latter unified modern China in 221 BC, and became a regular feature of virtually all subsequent Chinese dynasties. Indeed, the preparation of young people for a competitive standardized exam is one of the oldest and deepest traditions in Chinese culture, adopted many centuries before they became the norm in Western administrative states. Chinese rulers faced similar structural and environmental conditions to those of their early modern European counterparts, and invented comparable social institutions despite their physical separation and cultural differences.

So while liberal individualism may be the historically contingent by-product of Western civilization, it has proven to be highly attractive to people of varied cultures once they are exposed to the freedom it brings. Modern economic life, moreover, depends on individuals breaking free of the restrictive communal bonds that characterize traditional societies, and in recent years millions of people have sought to flee such places to jurisdictions that promise not just greater economic opportunity, but greater personal freedom.

The related charge that liberal states have failed to recognize groups is broadly wrong. Liberal states recognize and give legal status, and sometimes financial support, to a wide variety of groups. What they are more reluctant to do is to vest fundamental rights in involuntary groups based on fixed characteristics like race, ethnicity, gender, or inherited culture. There are good reasons for this reluctance: each of these groups encompass a wide variety of individuals whose interests and identities may be very different from that attributed to the group as a whole. There is also a serious problem with representation: who is it that speaks on behalf of African Americans, or women, or gay people as a category?

Multiculturalism can be a relatively neutral noun that simply describes the reality of diverse societies in which people of different cultural backgrounds live together. Individual autonomy often entails the choice of group identity, and liberal societies need to protect that freedom. In liberal societies like the United States, Australia, and Canada, big cities enjoy a huge degree of cultural diversity that adds richness and interest to life.

But there are types of cultural autonomy that are not consistent with liberal principles. A number of Muslim immigrant communities discriminate against women, gay people, and those who want to leave the faith, in ways that do not respect liberal rules about individual autonomy. The classic case of this is a Muslim family that wants to force their daughter into an arranged marriage against her will. In Europe, this has put the state in the position of having to decide between protecting the communal rights of the immigrant community, or the individual rights of the woman in question. Here it would seem that a liberal society would have no choice but to side with the woman, and restrict the autonomy of the group.

The charge that contract theory does not reflect the power balances between different social groups is true enough, but again these issues have been corrected in liberal societies over time. There was indeed a racial contract at America's founding, exemplified by the three-fifths clause of the US

Constitution that didn't count black people as full human beings. The document was a contract that represented a compromise between parties that wanted to preserve slavery, and others who wanted to abolish or at least restrict its extent. The moral issue of slavery would continue to bedevil American politics, and was, as Lincoln noted in his Second Inaugural address, the underlying cause of the Civil War. The amendments to the Constitution passed in the aftermath of the war changed the nature of the contract fundamentally. It took another hundred years for that contract to be fulfilled juridically, and the lingering effects of the original sin of slavery remain ever-present. Some contemporary race theorists argue that this racial contract remains in place, and that existing institutions continue to be premised on white supremacy.[14] But it is neither the fact nor the nature of the contract itself that is the driver of current racial inequities.

The charge that liberalism inevitably leads to neoliberalism and an exploitative form of capitalism ignores the history of the late nineteenth and twentieth centuries. In this period, working-class incomes rose over several generations, and income inequality as measured by Gini coefficients fell through the middle of the twentieth century. Virtually all advanced liberal societies had put into place extensive social protections and labor rights from the late nineteenth century onwards. Liberalism by itself is not a sufficient governing doctrine on its own; it needs to be paired with democracy so that there can be political corrections made to the inequalities produced by market economics. There is no reason to think that such corrections cannot occur within a broadly liberal political framework in the future.

The view that liberalism and capitalism were somehow

essentially linked to colonialism makes a fundamental methodological mistake by trying to cram complex, multicausal developments into a single monocausal theory. Sugar and cotton grown by slaves did play a role in the economic development of Britain and the United States. But there is a gigantic scholarly literature on why the West broke away from the rest of the world in terms of economic development, democratic government, and military power. In this account, climate, geography, culture, family structure, competition, and sheer luck played important roles. Colonialism and racism do not explain why other parts of the non-Western world like East Asia succeeded in doing something similar during the later twentieth and twenty-first centuries. Early theorists of capitalism like Adam Smith argued explicitly against the need for colonial domination as a route to prosperity, on the grounds that free trade was economically far more efficient. And indeed, the world as a whole has grown much richer following the dismantling of the world's colonial empires.

This has led critics of liberalism to charge that liberalism has simply replaced formal modes of domination with informal ones; free trade between countries of vastly different power is not really free. The decimation of India's indigenous textile industry when exposed to competition from British goods in the nineteenth century is often cited as an example. Yet against such cases, we need to look at the rise of East Asia, which was able to catch up to the West, and now threatens to overtake it in some sectors, precisely because it accepted the terms of the liberal global economy. There is today an enormous international development industry whose resource transfers from rich countries to poor ones have supported state budgets across sub-Saharan Africa. One may argue that these efforts have not been ultimately successful except in the domain of public health, but they are in no way morally equivalent to the Belgian king Leopold's efforts to strip resources from the Congo.

The final charge against liberalism concerns the checks and balances that liberal regimes place on the exercise of power, which then prevents radical redistribution of power and wealth from taking place. This charge is valid as far as it goes. An authoritarian country like China could make radical changes rapidly, as when Deng Xiaoping opened the economy to market forces after 1978. So rapid a change in fundamental economic institutions would be inconceivable in a constitutional republic like that of the United States. In some parts of the contemporary progressive left, there has been a revived interest in the writings of Carl Schmitt, the early twentieth-century legal theorist traditionally associated with the right who argued in favor of the exercise of discretionary executive power.[15]

But liberal constraints on power should be seen as a kind of insurance policy. Checks and balances are there to prevent autocratic abuses of power. The lack of constitutional constraints in China made possible not just Deng Xiaoping's reforms, but also the disastrous Great Leap Forward and Cultural Revolution under Mao. Lack of checks and balances is facilitating the centralization of dictatorship under Xi Jinping today. America's checks and balances limit the possibility of the kind of reforms desired by young progressives today, but they also protected the country from attempted abuses of power by Donald Trump. It is perfectly possible to change the institutional rules of a liberal democracy to, for example, eliminate the filibuster as an obstacle to passing legislation in Congress. I have argued elsewhere that America has become a "vetocracy" in which political decisions are extremely hard to make because of the large number of veto points that have accumulated in the American political system. But failure to restrict power altogether is always a dangerous proposition, because we do not know in advance the identity of future power holders.

It is true that historically liberal societies colonized other cultures, discriminated against racial and ethnic groups within their own borders, and assigned women to subordinate social roles. But saying that racism and patriarchy were intrinsic to liberalism is to essentialize historically contingent phenomena. The fact that self-proclaimed liberals endorsed illiberal ideas and policies in the past does not mean that the doctrine was incapable of acknowledging and correcting these mistakes, something that critical race theorist Charles Mills himself acknowledges.[16] Indeed, liberalism itself provided the theoretical justification for its own self-correction. It was the liberal idea that "all men are created equal" that allowed Abraham Lincoln to argue against the morality of slavery before the Civil War, and it was this same idea that animated the expansion of full citizenship to all people of color curing the Civil Rights era.

The final charge made by progressives against liberalism has to do with the modes of cognition closely associated with liberalism ever since the Enlightenment, which is that of modern natural science. It is in this domain that the threat to liberalism is the most acute today, so we will turn now to focus on a narrower set of institutions related to cognition and speech.

6

The Critique of Rationality

The critical theories attached to identity politics in the United States have produced a critique not just of liberal principles, but of the modes of discourse associated with it. It is in this realm that they are producing their most evident effect. In its more extreme versions, this critique denies the possibility of the liberal ideal of rational discourse altogether. This strand of thought runs from structuralism through post-structuralism, postmodernism, and ultimately to the many forms of contemporary critical theory. Like the critiques of liberalism noted in the last chapter, it begins with a number of true observations, but then is carried to unsupportable extremes. In the process, many of the arguments pioneered by the progressive left have drifted over to the populist right. When combined with modern communications technology, this critique lands us in a cognitive wasteland where, in Peter Pomerantsev's words, "nothing is true and everything is possible."[1]

From its earliest beginnings, modern liberalism was strongly associated with a distinctive cognitive mode, that of modern natural science. This mode assumes that there is an objective reality outside the human mind, which human beings can gradually understand and ultimately come to manipulate. The fountainhead of this approach was the philosopher René Descartes, who began with the most radical imaginable skepticism about the existence of that external reality, and progressively worked his way towards a structured system by which it could be apprehended. That apprehension would come to be based on empirical observation and an experimental method, pioneered by Francis Bacon, that sought to establish causality by controlling the observation of correlated events. This is the method upon which modern natural science is based, and is taught in every basic statistics course in the world today. Liberalism was thus strongly associated with the project of mastering nature through science and technology, and using the latter to bend the given world to suit human purposes.

Modern democracies are facing a deep cognitive crisis. The sociologist Max Weber distinguished facts from values and argued that rationality could only determine the former. While we might not be able to agree on a statement like "a human embryo is morally equivalent to an infant," we could agree on the truth or falsehood of a statement like "it is raining outside now." For many years now, modern societies have been living with moral relativism, which asserts the essential subjectivity of all value systems. Modern liberalism was in fact founded on the premise that people will not agree on the final ends of life or understandings of the good. Postmodernism, however, has moved us further, from moral to epistemic or cognitive relativism, in which even factual observation is regarded as subjective.

Jonathan Rauch notes that the approach to factual truth coming out of the liberal Enlightenment rests on trust in a social system that adheres to two rules: that no one gets the final say; and that knowledge has to be based on empirical evidence and not on the authority of the speaker.[2] To this we need to add a battery of techniques that seek either to verify empirical propositions through inductive reasoning, or falsify them through simple observation, à la Karl Popper. These techniques are known collectively as the scientific method. Knowledge about the outside world is a cumulative social process by which that method is applied. The process may be open-ended, and its conclusions are never more than probabilistically true. But that doesn't mean that some of our beliefs about how the world beyond our subjective consciousness operates are not better established than others.[3]

The rise of the scientific method was critical in liberalism's struggle against entrenched religion. The liberal Enlightenment understood itself as the victory of human reason over superstition and obscurantism. Apart from divine revelation, there were a variety of alternative premodern modes of cognition, such as the reading of hidden signs and symbols in nature, or the exploration of one's interior consciousness.[4] Modern natural science was able to defeat these alternative approaches ultimately because it could produce repeatable results. The manipulation of nature produced the modern economic world, where continuing growth through technological advance could be taken for granted. Scientific approaches to health led to huge increases in longevity; and technology conferred on states huge military advantages that could be used to defend or to conquer. Modern science, in other words, was strongly associated with power, perhaps symbolized to greatest effect by the mushroom cloud exploding over Hiroshima in August 1945.

Precisely because modern natural science was so intimately

associated with existing power structures, it engendered a prolonged critique that questioned whether its dominance was justified or whether it actually served true human flourishing.

The route to the critique of modern natural science began in an unlikely place, the writings of a late nineteenth-century Swiss linguist named Ferdinand de Saussure. Saussure argued that words did not necessarily point to an objective reality beyond the speaker's consciousness; rather, they were bound up in a binary relationship of *signifiant* ("signifier") and *signifié* ("signified"), in which the act of speaking itself was responsible for shaping the way that the apparently external world was perceived.[5] The signifiers were linked together in a system that reflected the consciousness of those who used the language, and therefore differed cross-culturally.

Saussure's ideas were expanded during the 1960s and 1970s by a series of French writers including the psychoanalyst Jacques Lacan, the literary critic Roland Barthes, and the *philosophe* Jacques Derrida. What they took away from Saussure was the notion of radical subjectivity: the external world that we think we perceive is actually created by the words we use in talking about it. Although Derrida criticized Saussure, the deconstructionism he inspired sought to demonstrate that all writers were unconsciously complicit in reflecting the social structures in which they were embedded.[6] You do not read Shakespeare or Goethe to extract the author's meaning or wisdom; rather, you expose how the author himself betrayed his own intentions or reflected the unjust power relationships of his time. Saussure and the structuralism that flowed from his writings did not make generalizations about the essential subjectivity of all language; deconstructionism did. The latter approach provided an intellectual justification for attacking the Western canon, the set of foundational books stretching from Homer and the Hebrew Bible up through Marx and Freud that had been the basis for countless Western civilization courses in America and Europe.

The forerunner of this approach was Friedrich Nietzsche, who argued that "there are no facts, only interpretations." But the thinker who systematized this line of thought and who influenced subsequent trends most powerfully was Michel Foucault. In a series of brilliant books, Foucault argued that the language of modern natural science was used to mask the exercise of power. The definition of madness and mental illness, the use of incarceration to punish certain forms of behavior, medical categorizations of sexual deviancy and other practices were not based on neutral empirical observation of a given reality. Rather, they reflected the interests of broader power structures that wanted to subordinate and control different classes of people.[7] The supposedly objective language of modern natural science encoded these interests in ways that hid the influence of the power holder; people were thereby unconsciously manipulated into affirming the dominance of certain ideas and the groups that stood behind them.

With Foucault, deconstructionism evolved into postmodernism, a more general critique of the cognitive modes that had for centuries been strongly associated with classical liberalism. This critique was easily incorporated into the different varieties of critical theory that proliferated in the American Academy from the 1980s onwards, and were put to use as methods of attacking the racial and gendered power structures of the time. Edward Said's 1978 book *Orientalism* made explicit use of Foucault's theory of power and language to attack prevailing academic approaches to cross-cultural studies, laying the groundwork for later postcolonial theorists who have denied the possibility of "objective" knowledge unconditioned by the identity of the knowledge producer.[8] The United States had a long history of racial hierarchy and injustice that could not help but permeate virtually all of its institutions, and postmodernism provided a ready-made framework for understanding these issues. Language and the power relationships it encoded remained central to this critique: the adjective "American" for example was typically loaded with numerous assumptions about the subject's race, gender, and cultural proclivities. Contemporary arguments over gender pronouns are only the latest manifestation of the sensitivity of identity groups to the way that language subtly and often unconsciously enforces power relationships.

Foucault's understanding of language not as a neutral pathway to objective knowledge but as an instrument of power thus explains some of the extreme sensitivity to the mere expression of words on the part of people who have absorbed his ideas. On many college campuses and elite cultural institutions today, people will complain that the simple use of certain words, whether verbally or in print, constitutes violence and makes them feel "unsafe" and subject to traumatic stress. Anyone who has experienced real violence will know that there is a big difference between being punched in the face and hearing certain unpleasant words articulated. But by Foucault's logic, the words themselves are expressions of power, and that power, it is asserted, can make people feel physically unsafe.

At the heart of the liberal project is an assumption about human equality: that when you strip away the customs and accumulated cultural baggage that each one of us carries there is an underlying moral core that all human beings share and can recognize in one another. It is this mutual recognition that makes possible democratic deliberation and choice.

This foundational idea has come under attack with the growing awareness of the complexities of identity. Individuals are not the autonomous agents of liberal theory; they are shaped by broader social forces over which they have no control. The "lived experience" of different groups, and particularly of those who have been marginalized by the mainstream society, is not perceived by those in the mainstream and cannot be shared by others with different life histories. Intersectionality is an acknowledgement of the fact that different forms of marginalization exist, and that their intersection creates new forms of prejudice and injustice. This is something that is understood in the first instance by people actually occupying those intersections, and not by the larger communities.[9] More broadly, knowledge about the world is not like a series of empirical facts that any observer can simply pick up and make use of. Knowledge is embedded in life experiences; knowing is not an abstract cognitive act but is intimately bound up with doing and acting and being acted upon.

It is impossible to simply reject many of these ideas, because they begin from observations that are indubitably true. Ideas that have been put forward as neutral, scientifically validated conclusions have indeed reflected the interests and power of those expressing them.

For example, the evolutionary biologist Joseph Heinrich has written about how social scientists researching human behavior have typically used what he labels WEIRD people as observational or experimental subjects—those who are Western, educated, industrialized, rich, and democratic. This research purports to describe universal human characteristics, but in fact reflects, Heinrich argues, culturally determined behavior and attitudes on issues like kinship, individualism, obligation, and government. WEIRD people, it turns out, are outliers when one looks at human behavior around the world more broadly.[10]

Similarly, the whole enterprise of neoclassical economics has presented itself as a neutral application of the scientific method to the study of economics. But the discipline has also reflected power relationships in the underlying society, particularly during its neoliberal phase, as described in earlier chapters. Among social scientists, economists have gone the furthest in trying to formalize their theories in abstract mathematical models, and in developing a rigorous empirical methodology to validate them. They are often characterized as suffering from "physics envy," hoping to turn their science into something on a par with the most abstract and mathematized of the natural sciences.

This did not prevent economics from falling prey to the attractions of power and money. Deregulation, strict defense of property rights, and privatization were pushed by wealthy corporations and individuals who created think tanks and hired big-name economists to write academic papers justifying policies that were in their private interests. This is not to accuse the vast majority of economists of outright corruption, though this may have happened in certain circumstances. Rather, it is a matter of what is labeled "intellectual capture": when you are trained in a certain manner, and all of your colleagues affirm the same set of beliefs, you tend also to accept that framework and endorse it, in perfect honesty. It didn't hurt that defense of these positions earned consulting fees and got one invited to conferences in nice resorts.

Many of the criticisms of modern natural science and the cognitive approaches associated with classical liberalism were therefore justified. But many versions of critical theory went far beyond attacks on specific misapplications of the scientific method to a broader critique of science as it had evolved since the Enlightenment. It argued that the search for human universals fundamental to liberalism was simply an exercise in power, one that embedded racism and patriarchy and sought to impose the ideas of one particular civilization on the rest of world. It was not possible for anyone to rise above the identities into which they were born, or to assume a higher perspective that cut across different identity groups. The feminist writer Luce Irigaray, for example, argued that in physics, solid mechanics was a masculine way of looking at the world, while fluid mechanics was a feminine one.[11] In place of the aspiration to accumulate a growing body of knowledge about the outside world through careful observation and deliberation, critical theory asserted a radical subjectivism that rooted knowledge in lived experience and emotion.

There was an element of conspiratorial thinking embodied in Foucault's critique of science as well. He argued that the nature of power had changed in the modern world. It was once an attribute used openly by monarchs, who could order the death of any of their subjects for disobeying a command. Modern power was exercised in a more subtle way; it structured institutions and the language used to regulate and talk about social life, things he labeled "biopower."[12] In his later writings, Foucault maintained that power pervaded virtually all activities, to the point that, critics argued, deprived his concept of any real explanatory power.[13] This nonetheless provided an argument that later critical theorists could use to explain how supposedly objective science was actually serving the interests of specific elite groups—white Europeans, men, "heteronormative" people, and the like.

Postmodernism and its critical theory offshoots have been around for a long time, and have been criticized and indeed ridiculed. A number of people working in this field, beginning with post-structuralists such as Lacan and Derrida, wrote in ways that seemed to deliberately obfuscate their thought and shield them from accountability for contradictions and weak logic.[14] It appeared to be an esoteric preoccupation confined to certain academic departments, but it has continued to provide a framework by which progressives can interpret the world. The murder of George Floyd in May 2020 provoked an enormous amount of well-justified anger, and protests across the United States against police violence. But it also spawned an anti-racist literature that has many echoes of past critiques.[15] In this reading, racism is not seen as an attribute of individuals, or as a policy problem to be solved. Rather, it is a condition that is said to pervade all American institutions and consciousness. Like Foucault's biopower, it reflects an underlying power structure of white supremacy that is embedded in language and that hides itself even from progressive people who believe themselves to be anti-racist.

The postmodernist critique of liberalism and its associated cognitive methods has now drifted over to the right. White nationalist groups today regard themselves as a beleaguered identity group. During the Covid epidemic, a much broader group of conservatives around the world used the same conspiratorial critique of modern natural science that had been pioneered by critical theory and the left. They have produced a mirror-image of Foucault's "biopower," arguing that the public health infrastructure recommending social distancing, mask-wearing, and shutdowns did not reflect "objective" science, but was rather motivated by hidden political motives.[16] The right-wing argument went much further than this, seeking to erode trust in the credibility of scientists generally, and in institutions making use of science. It is highly unlikely that contemporary conservatives from Donald Trump on down have read a word of the postmodernist theory they anathematize, but a number of intellectuals attracted to the movement, such as Andrew Breitbart and Peter Thiel, have done so. They have simply applied what started as a critique of the establishment to the contemporary progressive dominance of supposedly neutral institutions like academia and the mainstream media.[17]

The subversion of classical liberalism and its associated modes of cognition by progressive identity groups was undertaken on the assumption that such an effort would benefit groups that were historically marginalized under liberal institutions. Such groups would thus be accorded dignity and equal recognition in the manner promised by liberalism but never actually delivered.

In this respect, Friedrich Nietzsche was a far more honest and acute prophet of the likely impacts of the dethroning of liberal rationality than his early twenty-first-century critical theory followers. He argued that modern liberalism stood on a structure of assumptions ultimately underpinned by Christian morality. The Christian God once lived, but now that God was dead, the door was opened to the transvaluation of all values, including the value of equality. Nietzsche characterized Christianity as a slave religion, and praised the "blond beast" who had been tamed and domesticated by it. The principle that the weak should receive the same treatment as the strong was no more valid than the principle that the strong should rule the weak. Indeed, the only universal measure of value that remains is power, and the "will to power" that runs through all human activities. Translated into post-modernist terms, if Michel Foucault argues that the scientific method encodes the power and interests of hidden elites, then we have to ask what hidden power agenda drives Michel Foucault himself. If there are no truly universal values other than power, why should one want to accept the empowerment of any marginalized group, which will simply replace one expression of power with another?

This is precisely the argument that has been taken up by right-wing extremist groups in the United States today, who openly voice fears that they will be "replaced" by people of color. This is a grossly exaggerated fear, but it becomes plausible if we drop the liberal assumption that anyone, regardless of race, ethnicity, or gender, can participate on an equal basis in a broader liberal identity. These extremist groups are not fighting to preserve a liberal order, they are fighting to preserve their power in a zero-sum struggle with other ethnic groups.

While liberal societies agree to disagree about final ends, they cannot survive if they are unable to establish a hierarchy of factual truths. This hierarchy is created by elites of various sorts, who act independently of those holding political power. American courts are allowed to throw out filings that do not have a good-faith basis in fact and law, and can sanction lawyers who lie to them. Scientific journals will not publish studies that have not passed peer review, and will retract studies if they are shown to be fraudulent or based on bad evidence. Responsible journalists have systems for checking facts, and responsible media outlets will retract stories proven to be wrong or misleading. None of these systems is foolproof and all are capable of bias. But they are not deliberately engineered by the elites who oversee them to disempower or manipulate ordinary people.

There are thus two versions of modern identity politics. One version sees the drive for identity as the completion of liberal politics: historically dominant elites fail to appreciate the specific struggles of marginalized groups, and therefore fail to recognize their underlying common humanity. The goal of this form of identity politics is to win acceptance and equal treatment for members of the marginalized group as individuals, under the liberal presumption of a shared underlying humanity.

The other version of identity politics sees the lived experiences of different groups as fundamentally incommensurate; it denies the possibility of universally valid modes of cognition; and it elevates the value of group experience over what diverse individuals hold in common. This understanding of identity in time merges cleanly with a historical nationalism more commonly associated with the right. Nationalism originated in the early nineteenth century as a backlash against the universalizing claims of liberalism. Each nation had its own history and cultural traditions, nationalists argued, that needed to be preserved and cherished against a liberal politics that simply recognized people as amorphous individuals. The German Romantics, for example, attacked the scientific and empiricist approach of English liberals, and argued instead for truth built around feeling and intuition.

All of this suggests not that identity politics is wrong, but that we must return to a liberal interpretation of its aims. Liberalism with its premise of universal human equality needs to be the framework within which identity groups should struggle for their rights.

7

Technology, Privacy, and Freedom of Speech

One of classical liberalism's foundational principles concerns the protection of freedom of speech. This protection is written into the First Amendment of the American Bill of Rights, and has been enshrined in the basic laws of many liberal democracies, as well as in the Universal Declaration of Human Rights. Speech has an intrinsic moral value as the locus of thought and choice, as well as the practical value of permitting human beings to communicate in complex ways of which no other species is capable. Speech is necessary to the creation of institutions, which make possible coordination and cooperation across time and on a gigantic scale. Freedom of speech implies a freedom to think, and is the basis for all the other freedoms that liberal orders seek to protect.

As part of the broader attack on liberalism, freedom of speech has been contested on both the right and the left. It has also been severely challenged by changes in technology that provide new and untested channels through which societies can communicate.

There are two normative principles undergirding freedom of speech in a liberal society. The first has to do with the need to avoid artificial concentrations of power over speech.

The second is less obvious but equally necessary, which is the need for both government and citizens to respect a zone of privacy surrounding each member of the society. This zone can be defined in terms of a fundamental legal right as it is in Europe, but is better understood as a norm than a justiciable right because it should affect the private behavior of citizens toward one another and be seen as an extension of the virtue of tolerance. Both of these principles have been threatened by technological change in the way that we now communicate, as well as by other social developments such as political polarization.

Power over speech has been concentrated in several ways today. The first is the age-old one of authoritarian governments, or would-be authoritarians in ostensibly democratic countries, trying to monopolize and control speech. Classical liberalism is highly distrustful of this kind of state power, and indeed speech is usually the first target of any authoritarian regime. The current Chinese Communist Party exercises ever-tightening control over both legacy media and the internet; and Russia's Vladimir Putin has put all major media channels under his control or the control of his cronies. The internet has facilitated surveillance on an undreamed-of scale through the tracking and sensors that have become ubiquitous in daily life. China's social credit system merges surveillance with large-scale data mining and artificial intelligence, which allows the government to keep tabs on the thoughts and behaviors, both small and large, of its citizens.

The second threat comes not from governments, but from *private* control over legacy media and communications, and was pioneered by former Italian prime minister

Silvio Berlusconi. Berlusconi became a wealthy oligarch through his ownership of a large media empire, Mediaset, which had extensive properties in newspapers, publishing, and broadcasting. This control allowed him to become a celebrity in his own right, which he parlayed into the prime ministership in the early 1990s, just as Italy's post–Second World War political order was collapsing with the demise of the Socialist and Christian Democratic parties. Once in power, Berlusconi could use his newfound political influence to protect his business interests, and shield himself from criminal liability.

Berlusconi's success in combining media with political power has since then been widely imitated. While not a media baron himself, Vladimir Putin recognized early on the importance of bringing private media channels under his control, or under the control of his cronies. In the process he personally became one of the richest men in Russia, if not the world. Viktor Orbán in Hungary and Recep Tayyip Erdoğan in Turkey used their personal control of media channels to similarly cement their political power and family wealth. With the rise of the internet in the late 1990s, legacy media became less attractive as an investment, and many media properties were bought up by local oligarchs who saw them not so much as attractive business ventures but as routes into politics.[1] The country in which oligarchic control of legacy media has gone the furthest is Ukraine, where virtually all of the main radio and TV channels are controlled by one of seven oligarchs.

The third major threat to freedom of speech arises, paradoxically, from the sheer volume of speech that the internet has made possible. When the internet got going in the 1990s as a public communications channel there was a widespread belief that it would have a profoundly democratizing effect. Information was a source of power, and greater access to information would spread power more broadly. The internet would allow everyone to become their own publisher, bypassing legacy media's gatekeepers—publishers, editors, media corporations, and governments. The internet also permitted popular mobilizations, and greatly facilitated uprisings against authoritarian or corrupt regimes in Ukraine, Georgia, Iran, as well as those that took place during the Arab Spring. It allowed isolated individuals suffering abuse or persecution to find one another despite geographic constraints, and move towards collective action.

But as Martin Gurri observed, the new information universe in which digital media combined with legacy media began to overwhelm everyone with more information than they had ever had access to previously or could make sense of. As time passed it became evident that much of this information was of poor quality, false, or at times deliberately weaponized to achieve specific political purposes. While some empowered individuals, such as Wael Ghonim in Egypt, could help bring down an Arab dictatorship, others could also single-handedly spread misinformation about vaccines or voter fraud. The cumulative effect of this information explosion was to undermine the authority of existing hierarchies—governments, political parties, media corporations, and the like—that had previously been the narrow channels through which information was purveyed.[2]

Classic American First Amendment theory aims to constrain only the first of these sources of concentrated power over speech: the government. In the absence of state control, it is assumed there will be a marketplace of voices, and that, over time, good information will drive out bad in a process of democratic deliberation. A similar idea underlies European thinking on free speech, such as the priority that Jürgen Habermas gives to the "public sphere" in democratic theory. Like any product market, the marketplace for ideas works best if it is large, decentralized, and competitive.

There are serious problems with the classic theory. In the first place, not all voices in a democratic debate are in fact equal to one another. The scientific method's "constitution of knowledge" is decentralized, open-ended, and does not rely on any single source of authority to verify its findings. But in this system, knowledge accumulates based on empirical observation underpinned by a rational methodology for establishing causal relationships. It relies for its performance on a broad normative preference for empirical rigor. An individual citing anecdotes about the effects of a particular medical treatment on his relatives should not have the same standing as a scientific study reporting the results of a large-scale randomized trial. A partisan blogger asserting the opinion that a particular politician is highly corrupt should not have the same weight as an investigative journalist who has spent six months carefully going through that politician's financial records. Yet the internet makes these alternative views appear to be equally credible.

The idea that there is an intrinsic hierarchy to information is embedded in modern legal systems. In convicting an accused person of a criminal charge "beyond a reasonable doubt" (as US jurisprudence puts it), courts will always try to limit the impact of hearsay; that something has been asserted on the internet is not sufficient for it to be deemed legally admissible evidence, for example. Professional journalism also enforces a hierarchy of information, with requirements for verifying sources and being transparent about them.

This becomes an acute problem because the large internet platforms operate on a business model that prioritizes virality and sensationalism over any type of careful vetting of information. A salacious and false story could be spread by these digital platforms with a speed and on a scale that no legacy media source could ever hope to match. Network economies (i.e., the fact that networks become more valuable to their users the larger they are) guarantee that the power to distribute or suppress information becomes concentrated in the hands of just two or three gigantic internet platforms. Rather than dispersing power, the modern internet has concentrated it.

The standard model of human cognition underlying the liberal Enlightenment holds that human beings are rational: they observe an empirical reality external to themselves, make causal inferences about those observations, and are then able to act upon the world based on the theories they have developed. Jonathan Haidt and other social psychologists have suggested that in practice many people follow a very different cognitive model.[3] They do not begin with any kind of neutral observation of empirical reality. Rather, they begin with strong preferences for the reality they prefer, and use their considerable cognitive skills to select empirical data and devise theories that support that reality in a process labeled "motivated reasoning."

The internet platforms have made great use of motivated reasoning. They possess mountains of data about their users' preferences, which allows them to target content in very precise ways so as to maximize those users' interactions with them. No one forces users to behave in this manner; it appears to them as voluntary choice, but actually is based on a sophisticated behind-the-scenes manipulation on the part of the platforms. Rather than contributing to a social process in which new and diverse information is vetted, digested, and deliberated, the platforms tend to reinforce existing beliefs and preferences. They do this not out of any direct political motivation, but to enhance their own bottom lines, and in the process undermine the proper functioning of democratic deliberation.

The second principle that should govern speech in a liberal society is the need for both government and citizens to respect a zone of privacy surrounding each member of the society. In Europe, privacy has been inserted in the basic laws of many countries and for the EU as a whole as a fundamental right. Respect for privacy should apply not just to governments and large corporations, but to individuals in their behavior toward one another.

There are several reasons why protection of a zone of privacy is critical for liberalism to work. The first is derived directly from the nature of liberalism itself. If we understand liberalism to be a means of governing over diversity, we assume that there will be no consensus over substantive views of the good life. This does not mean that individuals need to abandon their moral commitments, but only that these commitments need to be observed in private life and not imposed on other people. Citizens of a liberal republic need to practice tolerance, which means respecting diversity and forswearing the urge to make other people conform to one's own deep beliefs. It is people's public persona—the way they behave towards other people—that should be of concern, and not the nature of their innermost beliefs.

Respecting other people's privacy may seem like an uncontroversial demand, but it is one that is oftentimes at odds with other principles, such as the idea that individual behavior should be transparent and that people should be held accountable for it. In recent years, there has been a tremendous push for greater transparency and accountability across the board. This demand begins with public institutions like legislatures and executive agencies, but has spread to the governance of private organizations as well, from the Catholic Church to the Boy Scouts to corporations and non-governmental organizations. Without transparency, there can be no accountability: corrupt officials, abusive leaders, child pornographers and sex traffickers can hide behind a veil of secrecy. Indeed, transparency is regarded by many people as an unqualified good, where more is always better than less.

While privacy and transparency can be complementary goods in certain circumstances, they are just as often at war with one another, and there is no liberal society that can be completely transparent or do away with the need for privacy. Deliberation and negotiation cannot exist in a fully transparent world. No one buying a house wants the seller to have access to their discussions with their realtor on their final offering price; no one will be honest in a debate over hiring or promotion if their candid views are made known to everyone including the candidate. So-called "Chatham House" rules are invoked in private meetings precisely to encourage participants to speak frankly. In the United States, a number of laws like the Federal Advisory Commission Act and the Government in the Sunshine Act were passed in the 1970s in the wake of the Watergate scandal. Along with 24/7 TV coverage of Congress, these mandated transparency rules have been widely blamed for the disappearance of deliberation in both the executive and legislative branches.[4]

The rise of the internet in conjunction with legacy broadcast media has severely eroded everyone's zone of privacy. Private views that previously would have been expressed in person or over the telephone are now mediated by electronic platforms, where they leave a permanent record. In China, it is the government that has access to this data, which it can use to control the behavior of its citizens. In democratic countries, it is the large internet platforms that have access to this data, and a company like Facebook (now Meta) uses what it knows about your most intimate thoughts and preferences to market things to you.

But the problem does not begin and end with the big platforms. Many users express what they believe are private views through email or to small groups of people on social media. Anyone receiving the message, however, can broadcast it to the rest of the world, and many people have gotten into trouble in recent years simply for speaking honestly in what they believed to be a private setting. There is, moreover, no statute of limitations on the internet; anything you say becomes part of a permanent public record that is extremely difficult to disavow subsequently.

These trends were all illustrated by the case of Donald McNeil, a veteran reporter for the *New York Times*. On a study trip to Peru with a group of high school students, McNeil was accused of using a racial epithet, not in his own name, but as a quotation, and more broadly of speaking in a way that some students interpreted as racist. The story became a sensation on social media, and led to a huge mobilization of outraged staffers at the newspaper who demanded an apology from McNeil and eventually forced his departure.[5]

Freedom of speech encompasses the right of private organizations to discipline and control what their members say and do when acting in their name. There are certainly things that McNeil could have said that would have appropriately led to his disciplining by the newspaper through an internal process. The problem here was the new standard for judging what constituted racist behavior. The *Times'* own editor Dean Baquet concluded that "it did not appear to me that his intentions were hateful or malicious"; but contemporary anti-racist activists have sought to divorce racism from intent. It is no longer sufficient for people to behave in a non-racist way; their private thoughts are said to be pervaded by hidden racism and need to be brought into line with the prevailing orthodoxy. The existence of social media meant that the *New York Times* could not deal with the problem quietly through its own internal processes, but saw the incident turn into a target of national debate. The McNeil case shows how privacy has been eroded through the confluence of several broader trends: first, the belief that transparency should extend to all forms of private behavior; second, the extreme sensitivity to language engendered by identity politics' conflation of language and power; and third, the technological ability to turn private words into public utterances.

In the United States, privacy is protected in certain

limited domains like health information, but there are no national laws protecting other forms of privacy that are comparable to Europe's General Data Protection Regulations (GDPR).[6] But as the McNeil example shows, formal regulation of privacy would be very hard to implement and would have to involve detailed state intervention in private communications that could easily have counterproductive consequences. Protection of privacy can rest on clear law, but is ultimately better accomplished through social norms that would respect the ability of fellow citizens to hold unpleasant or controversial views.

On the other hand, protection of privacy requires very different norms regarding public speech. Citizens need to observe standards of civility when talking to one another. A great deal of political speech in the United States today is not intended to engage people with other reasoned opinions; in many cases, it is designed to deliberately provoke opponents or stoke agreement on the part of like-minded people.

Freedom of speech is thus challenged both by concentrations of power that give certain actors great control over speech, and by the steady erosion of the zone of privacy that a liberal society seeks to protect. The deliberative function of freedom of speech has been weakened not just by excessive demands for transparency, but also by the rise of different kinds of fantasy worlds made possible by the shift of our social interactions to online communications.

In the United States in 2021, a significant part of the American right is living in a fantasy world in which Donald Trump won the November 2020 presidential election by a landslide, but had it stolen from him through massive fraud on the part of the Democrats. This has led to real world consequences like the storming of the Capitol on January 6, 2021 by a pro-Trump mob. It has also led to Republican politicians in states like Georgia, Texas, Florida, and Arizona passing laws designed to correct a nonexistent problem by restricting voter access and awarding themselves the right to override election results in future polls if they fail to return Republicans as winners. In the wake of the country's vaccine rollout in response to the Covid pandemic, many conservatives have turned against vaccination as a politically motivated government plot. A smaller but still significant number have signed on to even more outlandish conspiracy theories, like the QAnon narrative that the Democratic Party is part of an international ring of pedophiles.[7]

The spread of such narratives is tied directly to the rise of the internet. Right-wing paranoia was always present in American politics, from the Red Scare of the 1920s to Joseph McCarthy in the 1940s, but such conspiracy theories were generally exiled to the margins of the political spectrum.[8] Before the internet, information was controlled by a small number of broadcast channels and newspapers, making it very hard for a losing politician to claim electoral fraud in the absence of actual evidence. But the internet has provided an unlimited number of channels for disinformation to spread.

Normally, if one's preferred version of reality diverges sufficiently from actual reality, there will be an ultimate reckoning: one won't get the job, or arrive at the correct destination, or protect oneself from disease. But here, too, modern information technology has done many other things to interfere with people's cognitive landscapes. Increasingly, we do not directly interact with the outside world by touching, feeling, walking, or talking with other people. These activities are today more often mediated by screens that present us with avatars of that outside reality. Our social connections have spread far beyond the close circles of family and friends that we associated with a generation or two ago. Computer-generated simulations of reality have grown unbelievably realistic over time, and have blurred people's sense of what is real and what is a simulacrum. This is nowhere more so than in the online gaming world, or in the fantasist world of Hollywood superheroes, which occupy a huge and growing proportion of young people's time. In the gaming world, one does not have to live with the body or social identity one was born with, and there is little accountability for one's actions because people can remain anonymous. The fear of death, which normally forces us to limit risky behaviors like reckless driving or doing violence to other people, does not exist in the online world. This then constitutes the technological backdrop to the present-day situation in the United States, where those on either side of the current political divide do not simply disagree on ideologies and policy preferences, but see different versions of reality.

The progressive left has its own version of online fantasy. This version is far milder and less consequential than the right-wing one, and does not threaten the foundations of liberal democracy. But it does have consequences in terms of the left's ability to accomplish its own agenda.

As we have seen, the critical theory tradition associated with identity politics places extraordinary emphasis on words and language as signifiers of underlying power structures. This often turns into the mistaking of words for actual power. In venues like universities and the arts, there has been a massive expansion in the understanding of what constitutes harm to others. In some cases, the simple articulation of certain proscribed words is construed to be the equivalent of violence, so their banning is justified as a matter of physical safety.

The internet has provided people with an outlet for their feelings about social justice, while relieving them of the need to actually bring it about. Achieving social justice in a liberal democracy is a hard task: it begins with popular mobilization, which requires raising people's consciousness about injustice on issues like race, gender, disability, or other conditions of discrimination. Online activism is perfect for this. But it then requires moving from mobilization to action: someone must formulate policies and laws to remedy the situation; elections need to be contested, victories won, and governing majorities formed; legislators need to be persuaded to devote resources to solutions; policies need to be litigated through the courts, and then implemented on a large scale. Many of these stages require persuading fellow citizens who do not initially agree with the social justice issue at hand, which might in turn require adapting one's objectives to fit political reality.

The internet has allowed people to mistake speech acts for acts that affect outcomes in the real world. By blocking a speaker one believes to be racist, activists persuade themselves that they have actually struck a blow against racism. What they have done instead is simply shift the venue of speech, and made themselves the target of justifiable criticism from the right. Social media companies have cleverly created incentive systems that persuade people they are doing something important if they pile up "likes" or retweets, whereas in reality such measures are significant only within the closed environment of social media itself. This is not to say that social media cannot lead to meliorative outcomes in the real world. Most people, however, are satisfied with the simulacrum of reality that they get through their online interactions.

The attack on modern natural science and Enlightenment approaches to cognition began on the left, as critical theory exposed the hidden agendas of the elites who promoted them. This approach often denied the possibility of true objectivity, and valued instead subjective feelings and emotions as a source of authenticity. Skepticism has now drifted over to the populist right, who see elites using these same scientific cognitive modes not as techniques to marginalize minority communities, but rather to victimize the former mainstream. Progressives and white nationalists come together in valuing raw feeling and emotion over cold empirical analysis.[9]

A long-term solution to the problem of the alternative realities brought on by the internet and digital communications cannot be the abandonment of the principle of free speech through the use of power to simply shut down disfavored forms of speech, whether this is done by governments, corporations, or digital online mobs. Even if one agrees with the use of such power in the short run, or for a purpose like preventing the incitement of immediate violence, it should be clear that this kind of power is very dangerous and will inevitably be wielded by other actors with whom one disagrees over time. We need to restore liberalism's normative framework, including its approach to rationality and cognition. A critical norm is belief not in "science," which never speaks with a single, authoritative voice, but in a scientific method that is open-ended and dependent on empirical verification and falsification. Freedom of speech depends further on norms of civility and respect for other people's zones of privacy. It remains the case that there is an objective world out there beyond our subjective minds, and that if an alternative reality strays too far from it, it will be impossible to accomplish real-world goals, no matter how much we may want that alternative reality to be true. We can swallow the wrong color pill, but eventually we will wake up from the dream.

8

Are There Alternatives?

There are many legitimate criticisms to be made of liberal societies: they are self-indulgently consumerist; they don't provide a strong sense of community or common purpose; they are too permissive and disrespect deeply held religious values; they are too diverse; they are not diverse enough; they are too lackadaisical about achieving genuine social justice; they tolerate too much inequality; they are dominated by manipulative elites and don't respond to the wishes of ordinary people. But in each case, we need ask the question: what superior principle and form of government should replace liberalism? This challenge is meant in two distinct senses: normatively, are there alternative principles that should replace those that guide liberalism, and replace its universalism, premise of human equality, and dependence on law? And second, as a matter of practical politics, is there a way to get to an alternative political order that is realistic?

Let's begin with a more specific account of the discontents expressed by the political right. These center on something very fundamental to liberalism and have been raised repeatedly over the centuries during which liberalism has existed. Classical liberalism deliberately lowered the sights of politics, to aim not at a good life as defined by a particular religion, moral doctrine, or cultural tradition, but at the preservation of life itself in conditions where populations could not agree on what the good life was. This leaves liberal orders with a spiritual vacuum: they allow individuals to go their own way, and create only a thin sense of community. Liberal political orders do require shared values like tolerance and openness to compromise and deliberation, but these are not the strong bonds of a tightly knit religious or ethno-nationalist community. Liberal societies have often fostered the aimless pursuit of material self-gratification, a consumer society that is both hungry for status but never satisfied with what any given individual is able to achieve.

This vacuum is deplored by conservative intellectuals like Sohrab Ahmari and Adrian Vermeule, who associate liberalism with the destruction of religiously rooted standards of moral behavior. They have attacked precisely the expanding realm of individual autonomy noted in chapter 6. According to Ahmari, "The movement we are up against prizes autonomy above all, too; indeed, its ultimate aim is to secure for the individual will the widest possible berth to define what is true and good and beautiful, against the authority of tradition."[1] Adrian Vermeule posits an alternative system that moves beyond autonomy: "It is now possible to imagine a substantive moral constitutionalism that . . . is also liberated from the left-liberals' overarching sacramental narrative, the relentless expansion of individualistic autonomy."[2] Religious rules have been particularly important in regulating family life and sexual behavior. Christian conservatives have for long deplored the spread of abortion as an assault on the sanctity of life, as well as related practices like euthanasia. The rapid acceptance of homosexuality and gender fluidity by liberal societies in recent years has added to this discontent. More broadly, many religious conservatives see liberalism as promoting a general moral laxity in which individuals worship themselves, rather than any transcendent God or moral principle. While this view is associated with conservative Christians in the United States, it is also characteristic of conservative Jews, Muslims, Hindus, and people of other faiths.

Nationalists have a similar complaint to that of religious conservatives: liberalism has dissolved the bonds of national community and replaced it with a global cosmopolitanism that cares about people in distant countries as much as it cares for fellow citizens. Nineteenth-century nationalists based national identity on biology and believed that national communities were rooted in common ancestry. This continues to be a theme for certain contemporary nationalists such as Viktor Orbán, who has defined Hungarian national identity as being based on Hungarian ethnicity. Other contemporary nationalists like Yoram Hazony have sought to distance themselves from twentieth-century ethno-nationalism, arguing instead that nations constitute coherent cultural units that allow their members to share thick traditions of food, holidays, language, and the like.[3] Patrick Deneen has argued that liberalism constitutes a form of anti-culture that has dissolved all forms of pre-liberal culture, using the power of the liberal state to insert itself into and control every aspect of private life. Significantly, he and other conservatives have broken with economic neoliberals, and have been vocal in blaming market capitalism for eroding values of family, community, and tradition.[4] As a result, the twentieth-century categories that defined left and right in terms of economic ideology do not fit the present reality neatly, with right-wing groups being willing to countenance the use of state power to regulate both social life and the economy.

There is, of course, considerable overlap between religious and nationalist conservatives. Among the traditions that contemporary nationalists want to preserve are religious ones; thus the Law and Justice Party in Poland has been closely aligned with the Polish Catholic Church and has taken on many of the latter's cultural complaints about liberal Europe's support for abortion and gay marriage. Similarly, religious conservatives often regard themselves as patriots; this is certainly true for American evangelicals who formed the core of Donald Trump's Make America Great Again movement.

In some corners of the American right, unwillingness to tolerate diversity extends not just to fellow citizens of the wrong race, ethnicity, or religion, but to broad groups of people who actually constitute a majority of the population. According to Glenn Ellmers of the Claremont Institute,

> I'm really referring to the many native-born people— some of whose families have been here since the Mayflower—who may technically be citizens of the United States but are no longer (if they ever were) *Americans*. They do not believe in, live by, or even like the principles, traditions, and ideals that until recently defined America as a nation and as a people. It is not obvious what we should call these citizen-aliens, these non-American Americans; but they are something else.[5]

For this writer, the test of being a "true" American is whether one voted for Donald Trump in 2020, which makes the more than 80 million voting for Biden "non-Americans."

There is a separate conservative critique of liberalism that is related less to the substance of liberal policies than to the procedures by which they were brought into existence. Liberalism is rooted in law, and protects the autonomy of judges and the courts. While judges theoretically interpret laws passed by democratically elected legislators, they have at times bypassed the latter and promoted policies that allegedly reflect their own preferences and not those of voters. Christopher Caldwell has argued that the Civil Rights revolution of the 1960s was brought about largely by judges, and has been expanded by the courts to encompass other areas of discrimination like women's rights and gay marriage. This has led, in his view, to an alternative constitutional order from the one originally envisioned by the Founders in 1789, that is, one in which it is not democratic majorities that make important decisions but rather unelected judges.

A parallel conservative complaint is that rules regarding socially sensitive topics like gender roles and sexual orientation have been promulgated by an unaccountable administrative state, often working at the behest of similarly unaccountable judges. In the United States, many public policies are formulated by states and local school boards, which are able to set curricula through bureaucratic fiat rather than legislative mandates. At times, when these rules are put up for popular choice through referenda, they are defeated (as in the case of California's Proposition 8 banning gay marriage); the results can nonetheless be disregarded as a result of subsequent court decisions.

While judicial activism is not as big an issue in Europe as it is in America, there are still loud complaints on the right about the power of the courts to override popular choice. The European Court of Human Rights and the European Court of Justice have, for example, issued binding decisions about the status of refugees that has restricted the ability of EU member states to deal with this sensitive issue on their own. Following the Syrian migrant crisis in 2014, this fueled populist resentment against European institutions, and was one factor contributing to Britain's 2016 vote to leave the European Union. The European right has an even bigger problem with EU bureaucracy, which is far more powerful than its American counterpart in the domain of economic policy, and only weakly subject to any kind of direct democratic accountability.

The substantive conservative critique of liberalism—that liberal societies provide no strong common moral horizon around which community can be built—is true enough. This is indeed a feature and not a bug of liberalism. The question for conservatives is whether there is a realistic way to roll back the secularism of contemporary liberal societies and reimpose a thicker moral order.

Some conservatives may hope that their societies could return to imagined Christian moral order. But modern societies are far more diverse religiously today than at the time of Europe's religious wars in the sixteenth century. There are not just competing religions and religious sects, but deep divisions between religious and secular people, and these have produced sharp polarizations in Poland, Israel, and in the United States. There has been a broad decline in the United States over the past decade of young people professing belief in any established religion, with the US thereby following Europe towards secularism. The idea of rolling back the clock and restoring a shared moral horizon defined by religious belief is a practical non-starter. Those like Prime Minster Modi who hope to effect this kind of restoration are inviting the kind of oppression and communal violence that he oversaw when he was Chief Minister of the state of Gujarat.

If such a rollback cannot be accomplished by persuasion, some conservative intellectuals have flirted with the idea of overtly authoritarian government. Harvard law professor Adrian Vermeule, for example, has argued in favor of what he calls "common good constitutionalism":

> This approach should take as its starting point substantive moral principles that conduce to the common good, principles that officials (including, but by no means limited to, judges) should read into the majestic generalities and ambiguities of the written Constitution. These principles include respect for the authority of rule and of rulers; respect for the hierarchies needed for society to function . . .

He goes on to argue that common good constitutionalism's "main aim is certainly not to maximize individual autonomy or to minimize the abuse of power (an incoherent goal in any event), but instead to ensure that the ruler has the power needed to rule well."[6] Some conservative writers have suggested that Hungary's Viktor Orbán or Portugal's last dictator Antonio Salazar might serve as role models for future American leaders.[7] On the extreme right, there has been flirtation with violence as a way of stopping progressivism. The United States has always been awash in gun ownership, and the pandemic year 2020 saw a huge explosion in weapons purchases. Increasingly, justifications for gun ownership have turned from sports and hunting to the need to stand up to tyrannical governments, which for this group would include any administration controlled by Democrats.

It is possible to imagine some very ugly scenarios unfolding in the United States surrounding future contested elections, though it still seems extremely unlikely that armed rebellion will ever succeed in the country. Nor does it seem likely that Americans will ever accept overtly authoritarian government of the sort suggested by Vermeule. In recognition of this reality, conservative writers like Patrick Deneen and Rod Dreher have recommended retreat into small communities or even monasticism, in which like-minded believers could practice their beliefs shielded from the larger currents in liberal society.[8] There is nothing about contemporary American liberalism that is preventing them from doing this today; they are not positing an alternative to liberalism so much as taking advantage of liberalism's intrinsic openness to diversity.

The conservative procedural complaint about the role of unaccountable courts and bureaucracies pushing unpopular cultural agendas reflects a real problem for democratic choice. But once again, the complaint addresses a feature of liberalism with important historical roots. No *liberal* democracy grants untrammeled power to democratic majorities, because the founders of liberalism understood that the people themselves could make bad choices. This was particularly true of the American founders, who spent considerable time worrying about the excesses of democracy and designed a complex system of checks and balances to limit full democratic choice. Christopher Caldwell argues that the Civil Rights revolution of the 1960s ushered in a new constitutional order where courts could routinely override popular choice, but this is a serious misunderstanding of both the nature of the system and of American history.

The central issue confronting Americans after the founding was that of race. In the antebellum South, overwhelming majorities of voters supported the institution of slavery, at a time when the franchise was limited to white males. In his debates with Abraham Lincoln, Stephen Douglas argued for the primacy of democratic choice: he professed to not care whether the people voted slavery up or down; what was important was that their will be respected. Lincoln's response to this argument was to say that there were more important principles at stake than democracy, namely, the premise that "all men are created equal" contained in the Declaration of Independence. Slavery contravened this principle; it was wrong whether or not democratic majorities supported it.

Because of the choices made by Southern voters, the ending of slavery could not be brought about by democratic means, but required a bloody civil war to accomplish. Nor was democracy sufficient to end legal segregation and Jim Crow laws a century later. Majorities of white voters in the South supported continued segregation and could not be persuaded otherwise. The heavy use of courts and bureaucracies instead of legislatures during the Civil Rights era needs to be seen in the context of the country's racial history, in which voters themselves have not always chosen liberal politics.

It is not clear that Caldwell has a realistic alternative to the ills he describes. His argument about how liberalism overturned America's original constitution implies that he would like to go back to the situation before *Brown v. Board of Education*, in which democratic majorities could vote to restrict the fundamental rights of certain classes of citizens. What is far more realistic is for future courts and administrative agencies to exercise greater restraint in making decisions that infringe on the prerogatives of legislatures. In the US, the former have discovered new fundamental rights, while the latter have expanded simple legislative language banning racial and gender discrimination into hundreds of pages of detailed guidelines regarding the ways in which schools and universities should regulate sexual relations. Laws necessarily need to evolve in response to changing conditions, and courts and administrative agencies have a role in promoting these adjustments when legislatures are slow to act. But if they get too far ahead of public opinion, they risk de-legitimizing themselves. By allowing themselves to be used as a means of leapfrogging the legislative process, courts and agencies have been made the targets of intense backlash and politicization.

The critique of liberalism by those on the progressive left are similarly both substantive and procedural. The substantive complaint is that huge inequalities based on class, race, gender, sexual orientation, and the like have been present for decades. Mainstream politicians have learned to live with them, because educated professionals could build decent lives for themselves while walling themselves off from the rest of society. Following the Reagan-Thatcher revolution of the 1980s, many politicians of the left, from Bill Clinton and Tony

Blair to Barack Obama, shifted right and accepted neoliberal arguments about the need for market solutions, austerity, and incrementalism. Problems like police violence against African Americans were swept under the rug, even as outcome gaps between racial groups remained intractable or even increased. New problems like climate change have created huge inter-generational conflicts and could not be addressed in a serious way because of the power of entrenched actors like fossil fuel companies and conservative voters who don't believe in the reality of climate change. Liberal incrementalism has thus been a complete failure in coming up with solutions that rise to the level of the challenges that society faces.

These substantive critiques then lead to procedural com-plaints that are the source of tension between many Gen Z activists and their elders born in the baby boom generation. Liberal democracies are built around complex rules that require deliberation and compromise, and which often serve to block more radical forms of change. In a highly polar-ized country like the United States, this has meant that an evenly divided Congress could not agree on straightforward things like annual budgets, much less on sweeping new social policies to address issues like racial inequality or poverty. Indeed, over time, the rules have gotten more restrictive, as in the case of the routine use of the filibuster that requires unobtainable supermajorities in order to pass important legislation. This is why abolishing the filibuster has risen to the top of progressive priorities under the Biden administra-tion. These substantive and procedural complaints led many younger progressive activists to argue that it was not specific policies or leaders that had failed, but the system itself that was rigged against fundamental social change.

What would a progressive left-wing alternative to liberalism look like? Many American conservatives have convinced themselves that they are already living in a nightmare world in which a tyrannical "far left" state is trampling on their rights. They imagine a world in which the government moves seamlessly from mandating masks and vaccines to meet a health emergency, to one in which jackbooted thugs go door to door to forcibly take away people's guns and Bibles. According to authors like Patrick Deneen, today's overarching progressive consensus has already eviscerated all prior cultural traditions, implying that conservatives like himself have been silenced and no longer have a voice.

A more realistic picture of what a progressive post-liberal society would look like requires a bit more nuance. Unlike the right, very few people on the left are toying with the idea of overtly authoritarian government. To the contrary, the extreme left tends to be anarchist rather than statist. In left-leaning cities like Portland and Seattle, activists sought to create police-free areas like the latter's Capitol Hill Autonomous Zone, and have pushed for defunding police departments around the country. These policies have proven to be self-defeating: these autonomous zones have been plagued by crime and drug use, and the idea of defunding the police has become a huge albatross around the necks of more centrist Democratic politicians.

A more likely scenario for a progressive post-liberal society would be one which saw a vast intensification of existing trends. Considerations of race, gender, gender preference, and other identity categories would be injected into every sphere of everyday life, and would become the primary considerations for hiring, promotion, access to health, education, and other sectors. Liberal standards like color-blind meritocracy would take a back seat to overt preferences based on race and gender. While the use of affirmative action in the United States has up to now been limited by Supreme Court decisions like *Regents of the University of California v. Bakke*, this could change, and identity categories could be written into law. There would be big changes as well in the way that a post-liberal society related to the outside world. Such a society might decide to simply give up on efforts to manage borders, and put in place an open-ended asylum system. Driven by global threats like climate change, there could be much more deference given in law and policy to decisions made by international actors rather than by domestic courts and legislatures. Citizenship could be further watered down and become essentially meaningless by granting non-citizens the right to vote.

In the economic sphere, it is not clear that the progressive agenda would necessarily be post-liberal. Politicians like Bernie Sanders are not calling for the abolition of private property or a return to central planning; rather, they seek a very expansive form of social democracy that has been tried, with varying success, in other liberal societies. The government would provide generous social services, pay for higher education, fund health care, guarantee jobs and minimum incomes, regulate if not nationalize the financial system, and massively shift investment towards preventing climate change. All of this would be paid for by equally massive new taxes on the wealthy, or, as per modern monetary policy, through the time-tested mechanism of printing money.

It does not appear at this moment that anything like the full progressive agenda is likely to be realized. While greater economic redistribution appears to be reasonably popular among voters, there are strong limits to the appeal of the cultural part of the agenda. Polarization in the United States has not been symmetric. On the right, a substantial majority of conservative voters have shifted to what had once been regarded as fringe positions, centering on conspiracy theories of voter fraud and vaccines. Left-of-center voters by contrast remain much more diverse. A more extreme progressive wing has emerged since the mid-2010s, though at this juncture it does not represent anything like the dominant view within the Democratic Party. Thus the Overton window of American politics has widened in recent years, and overt illiberalism has been much more openly expressed on both the right and left. Neither extreme proposes a realistic alternative to classical liberalism, but both have been able to chip away at liberal ideals and to discredit those who seek to maintain them.

To paraphrase what Winston Churchill once said about democracy, liberalism is the worst form of government, except for all the others. This does not make for a rousing endorsement of classical liberalism; for that, we must look to other sources.

9

National Identity

Another discontent generated by liberal societies is their frequent inability to present a positive vision of national identity to their citizens. Liberal theory has great difficulties drawing clear boundaries around its own community, and explaining what is owed to people inside and outside that boundary. This is because the theory is built on top of a claim of universalism. As asserted in the Universal Declaration of Human Rights, "All human beings are both free and equal in dignity and rights"; further, "Everyone is entitled to all the rights and freedoms set forth in this Declaration, without distinction of any kind, such as race, colour, sex, language, religion, political or other opinion, national or social origin, property, birth or other status." Liberals are theoretically concerned with violations of human rights no matter where in the world they occur. Many liberals dislike the particularistic attachments of nationalists, and believe that they are "citizens of the world."

So how is the claim of universalism to be reconciled with the division of the world into nation-states? There is no clear liberal theory as to how national boundaries are to be drawn. This has led to intra-liberal conflicts over the separatism of regions like Quebec, Scotland, and Catalonia, as well as disagreements over the proper treatment of immigration and refugees.

If one were to construct such a theory, it would have to go something like this. All societies need to make use of force, both to preserve internal order and to protect themselves from external enemies. A liberal society does this by creating a powerful state, but then constraining that power under a rule of law. The state's power is based on a social contract between autonomous individuals who agree to give up some of their rights to do as they please in return for the state's protection. It is legitimated both by the common acceptance of law and, if it is liberal democracy, through popular elections.

Liberal rights are meaningless if they cannot be enforced by a state, which, by Max Weber's famous definition, is a legitimate monopoly of force over a defined territory. The territorial jurisdiction of a state necessarily corresponds to the area occupied by the group of individuals who signed on to the social contract. People living outside that jurisdiction must have their rights respected, but not necessarily enforced by that state.

States with delimited territorial jurisdiction therefore remain critical political actors, since they are the only ones able to make legitimate use of force. In today's globalized world, power is exercised by a wide variety of bodies, from multinational corporations to non-profit groups to terrorist organizations to supranational bodies like the European Union or the United Nations. The need for international cooperation has never been more evident, from issues like global warming to fighting pandemics to regulating air safety. But it remains the case that one particular form of power, the ability to enforce rules through the threat or actual use of force, remains under the control of national states. Neither the European Union nor the International Air Traffic Association deploys its own police or army to enforce the rules they set. If rules are violated, they still depend ultimately on the coercive capacity of the nations that empowered them. There is today a large body of international law, such as the European Union's *acquis communautaire*, that in many domains displaces national-level law. But international law continues in the end to rely on national-level enforcement. When EU member states disagree on important matters of policy, as they did during the euro crisis of 2010 or the migrant crisis of 2014, ultimate outcomes were decided not by European law, but by the relative power of member states. Ultimate power, in other words, continues to be the province of national states, which means that control of power at this level remains critical.

There is thus no necessary contradiction between liberal universalism and the need for nations. While human rights may be a universal normative value, enforcement power is not; it is a scarce resource that is necessarily applied in a territorially delimited way. Liberal states are perfectly justified in granting different levels of rights to citizens and noncitizens, because it does not have the resources or the writ to protect rights universally. All persons on the state's territory are due the equal protection of the law, but only citizens are full participants in the social contract with special rights and duties, in particular the right to vote.

The fact that nations remain the locus of coercive power should make us cautious about proposals to create new supranational bodies and to delegate such power to them. We have several hundred years of experience in learning how to constrain power at a national level through legal and legislative institutions, and how to balance power such that its use reflects general interests. We have no idea how to create such institutions at a global level, where for example a global court or legislature would be able to constrain arbitrary decisions of a global executive. The European Union is the most serious effort to do this at a regional level; the result is an awkward system characterized by excessive weakness in some domains (fiscal policy, foreign affairs) and excessive power in others (economic regulation). Europe at least has a certain common history and cultural identity that do not exist at a global level.[1]

Nations are important not just because they are the locus of legitimate power and instruments for controlling violence. They are also a singular source of community. Liberal universalism at one level flies in the face of the nature of human sociability. We feel the strongest bonds of affection for those closest to us, such as friends and family; as the circle of acquaintance widens, our sense of obligation inevitably attenuates. As human societies have grown larger and more complex over the centuries, the boundaries of solidarity have expanded dramatically from families and villages and tribes to entire nations. But few people love humanity as a whole. For most people around the world, the nation remains the largest unit of solidarity to which they feel an instinctive loyalty. Indeed, that loyalty becomes a critical underpinning of the state's legitimacy, and thus its ability to govern. We see the disastrous consequences of societies with weak national identity all over the world today, from struggling developing states like Nigeria or Myanmar, to failed states like Syria, Libya, or Afghanistan.[2]

This argument may seem similar to ones made by Yoram Hazony in his 2018 book *The Virtue of Nationalism*, where he argues for a global order based on the sovereignty of nation-states.[3] He has a point, in warning against the tendency of liberal countries like the United States to go too far in seeking to remake the rest of the world in their own image. But he is wrong in assuming that nations are clearly demarcated cultural units, and that a peaceful global order can be built by accepting them as they are. Today's nations are social constructions that are the by-products of historical struggles, often involving conquest, violence, forced assimilation, and the deliberate manipulation of cultural symbols. There are better and worse forms of national identity, and societies can exercise agency in choosing among them.

In particular, if national identity is based on fixed characteristics like race, ethnicity, or religious heritage, then it becomes a potentially exclusionary category that violates the liberal principle of equal dignity. So while there is no *necessary* contradiction between the need for national identity and for liberal universalism, there is nonetheless a powerful potential point of tension between the two principles. Under these conditions, national identity can turn into aggressive and exclusive nationalism, as it did in Europe during the first part of the twentieth century.

For this reason, liberal societies normatively should not recognize groups based on fixed identities like race, ethnicity, or religious heritage. But there are times when this becomes inevitable, and liberal principles fail to apply. There are many parts of the world in which ethnic and religious groups have occupied the same territory for generations and have their own thick cultural and linguistic traditions. In many parts of the Middle East, the Balkans, and South and Southeast Asia, ethnic or religious identity is de facto an essential characteristic for most people, and assimilating them to a broader national culture is highly unrealistic. It is possible to organize a form of liberal politics around cultural units; India for example recognizes multiple national languages and has in the past permitted its states to set their own policies with regard to education and legal systems. Federalism and devolution of powers to subnational units is often necessary in such diverse countries. Power can be formally allocated to different groups defined by cultural identity in a structure called "consociationalism" by political scientists. While this has worked reasonably well in the Netherlands, the practice has been disastrous in places like Lebanon, Bosnia, and Iraq, where identity groups see themselves locked in a zero-sum struggle against one another. In societies where cultural groups have not yet hardened into self-regarding units, it is therefore much better to deal with citizens as individuals rather than as members of identity groups.

On the other hand, there are other aspects of national identity that can be adopted voluntarily and therefore shared more broadly, from literary traditions, shared historical narratives and language, to food and sports.

Quebec, Scotland, and Catalonia are all regions with distinct historical and cultural traditions, and all include nationalist partisans seeking complete separation from the country to which they are linked. There is little doubt that they would continue to be liberal societies respecting individual rights were they to separate, as the Czech Republic and Slovakia did after they became separate countries. This is not to say that separation is desirable, but only that it need not contradict liberal principles. There is a big hole in liberal theory regarding how to deal with such demands and how to define the national boundaries of states that are fundamentally liberal. Outcomes have been determined less on the basis of principle than as a result of the push and pull of various pragmatic economic and political considerations.

National identity represents obvious dangers, but also an opportunity. National identity is a social construct, and it can be shaped to support rather than undermine liberal values. Nations historically have been molded out of diverse populations, who can feel a strong sense of community based on political principles or ideals rather than ascriptive group categories. The United States, France, Canada, Australia, and India are all countries that in recent decades have sought to construct national identities based on political principles rather than race, ethnicity, or religion. The US has gone through a long and painful process redefining what it meant to be an American, progressively removing barriers to citizenship based on class, race, and gender, in a process that has seen setbacks and is still not complete. In France, construction of national identity began with the French Revolution's Declaration of the Rights of Man and of the Citizen, which established an ideal of citizenship based on common language and culture. Both Canada and Australia in the mid-twentieth century were countries with dominant white majority populations and restrictive laws regarding immigration and citizenship, like the latter's notorious "White Australia" policy. Both reconstructed their national identities on non-racial lines after the 1960s, and, like the United States, opened themselves up to massive immigration. Today, both of these countries have higher levels of foreign-born populations than does the US, with little of America's polarization and white backlash.

Nonetheless, we should not underestimate the difficulty of forging a common identity in sharply divided democracies. We often forget the fact that most contemporary liberal societies were built on top of historical nations whose understandings of national identity had been forged through illiberal methods. France, Germany, Japan, and South Korea were all nations before they became liberal democracies; the United States, as many have noted, was a state before it became a nation.[4] The process of defining that nation in liberal political terms has been a long, arduous, and periodically violent one, and even today is being challenged by people on both left and right with sharply competing narratives about the country's origins.

If liberalism were to be seen as nothing more than a mechanism for peacefully managing diversity without a broader sense of national purpose, that could be considered a grave political weakness. People who have experienced violence, war, and dictatorship long to live in a liberal society, as Europeans did in the period after 1945. But as people get used to a peaceful life under a liberal regime, they tend to take that peace and order for granted, and start longing for a politics that will direct them to higher ends. In 1914, Europe had been free of devastating conflict for nearly a century, and masses of people were happy to march off to war despite the enormous material progress that had occurred in the interim.

We are perhaps at a similar point in human history, where the world has been free from large-scale interstate war for three-quarters of a century, and has, in the meantime, seen a massive increase in global prosperity that has produced equally massive social change. The European Union was created as an antidote to the nationalism that had led to the world wars, and in that respect has been successful beyond all hopes. Yet popular expectations have risen faster still. Young people are not grateful to the EU for creating peace and prosperity; rather, they chafe against its petty bureaucratic impositions. The weak sense of community at the core of liberalism becomes a heavier burden under these conditions.

There is much more to a positive vision of liberal national identity than successful management of diversity and the absence of violence. Liberals have tended to shy away from appeals to patriotism and cultural tradition, but they should not. National identity as a liberal and open society is something of which liberals can be justly proud, and their tendency to downplay national identity has allowed the extreme right to claim this ground. The privileges accorded to citizens have been steadily eroded by courts in Europe and the United States in recent decades, and even the remaining distinction between citizen and non-citizen, the right to vote, has been challenged.[5] Citizenship should convey a two-way bargain conveying acceptance of the social contract, and should be a point of pride. The promise of a liberal American identity was captured by novelist Michael Shara, in thoughts attributed to Col. Joshua Lawrence Chamberlain, the Union officer whose actions decided the battle of Gettysburg during the Civil War:

[Chamberlain] had grown up believing in America and the individual and it was a stronger faith than his faith in God. This was the land where no man had to bow. In this place at last a man could stand up free of the past, free of tradition and blood ties and the curse of royalty and become what he wished to become . . . The fact of slavery upon this incredibly beautiful new clean earth was appalling, but more even that that was the horror of Old Europe, the curse of nobility, which the South was transplanting to new soil . . . He was fighting for the dignity of man and in that way he was fighting for himself.[6]

Historically, liberal societies have been engines of economic growth, creators of new technologies, and producers of vibrant arts and culture. This has occurred precisely *because* they were liberal. The list would begin with ancient Athens, which was celebrated by Pericles in the following words:

We have a form of government . . . [which] is called a democracy. Wherein, though there be an equality amongst all men in point of law for their private controversies, yet in conferring of dignities one man is preferred before another to public charge, and that according to the reputation, not of his house, but of his virtue; and is not put back through poverty for the obscurity of his person, as long as he can do good service to the commonwealth. And we live not only free in the administration of the state, but also with one another void of jealousy touching each other's daily course of life; not offended at any man for following his own humour . . .[7]

The city states of northern Italy, like Florence, Genoa, and Venice, were oligarchies rather than democracies, but far more liberal than the centralized monarchies and empires that surrounded them, and from the Renaissance on became centers of art and thought. The liberal Dutch celebrated a Golden Age in the seventeenth century, and liberal Britain was the inventor of the Industrial Revolution. Liberal Vienna was home to Gustav Mahler, Sigmund Freud, and Hugo von Hofmannstahl, until it went into decline in the early twentieth century with the rise of German and other nationalisms. And the liberal United States in turn became the chief producer of global culture, from jazz and Hollywood to hip-hop, Silicon Valley and the internet, over the decades that it welcomed refugees from closed societies.

It is precisely a liberal society's ability to incubate innovation, technology, culture, and sustainable growth that will determine the geopolitics of the future. China under Xi Jinping has argued that it can become the world's dominant power under authoritarian conditions, and that the West, and particularly the United States, is in a state of terminal decline. What we do not know at present is whether this unfree political and economic model will be able to generate innovation and growth down the road, or will produce anything like an appealing global culture. Much of China's amazing growth story over the past four decades has been the product of its own flirtation with liberalism, the opening up of the Chinese economy that began with Deng Xiaoping's reforms in 1978, and the creation of a vibrant private sector. It is that private sector and not the country's lumbering state-owned enterprises that have been responsible for most of its hi-tech growth. China today is widely admired for its economic success and technological prowess. Its unfree social model is much less widely respected, and there are not millions of people longing to become Chinese citizens.

The unanswered question for the future is whether liberal societies can overcome the internal divisions that they themselves have created. What started out as an institutional mechanism to govern over diversity has spawned new forms of diversity that threaten those very mechanisms. So liberal societies will have to course correct if they are to compete with the world's rising authoritarian powers.

10

Principles for a Liberal Society

This book has tried to lay out the theoretical grounding of classical liberalism, and some of the reasons why it has generated discontents and opposition. If liberalism is to be preserved as a form of government, we need to understand the sources of these discontents. Such an understanding could yield a long laundry list of policy responses that might mitigate present-day resentments and insecurities, on topics from unemployment, health policy, and taxation to policing, immigration, and the regulation of the internet. Rather than doing that, I want to outline some general principles that should guide the formulation of more specific policies, principles that flow from the underlying theory.

Many of these principles will apply particularly to the United States. The US has for long been the world's leading liberal power, and in years past has been a "beacon of liberty" for many people around the world. I have argued elsewhere that American institutions have decayed over time, becoming rigid and hard to reform, and are suffering from capture by elites. When its complex constitutional structure of checks and balances has combined with growing political polarization, its institutions have become gridlocked and have failed to confront many basic governing tasks like passing yearly budgets. This is a condition I labeled "vetocracy."[1] If the US does not fix its underlying structural problems, it will not be able to compete effectively with the world's rising authoritarian powers. Many of the problems seen in the United States affect other liberal democracies as well, so America's ability to articulate and defend liberal principles may have broader application.

While classical liberalism may be understood as a means of governing over diversity, both the nationalist-populist right and the progressive left have problems with accepting the actual diversity that exists in their society. The hard core of the nationalist-populist right are what one would have to label ethno-nationalists, and were heavily represented among the rioters who stormed the US Capitol on January 6, 2021. The diversity that they fear is related to categories like race, ethnicity, gender, religion, and sexual orientation. These fears are driven by the changing demographic makeup of the United States, and the possibility that people like themselves will be "replaced" by non-white immigrants, or by militantly secular progressives whose numbers in urban America are steadily growing.

The challenge facing American conservatives today is not different from that faced by other conservatives historically, who have perpetually had to deal with shifting demographics and social change. In nineteenth- and early twentieth-century Europe, the main social base of conservative parties in Britain and Germany were landowners dependent on the existing social hierarchy, as well as certain aristocratic and middle-class groups who saw industrialization as a threat to their way of life. Every society was undergoing rapid social change as peasants left the countryside and urban populations grew. Those urban populations were increasingly mobilized; trade unions were beginning to form, as well as socialist and communist parties built on top of this new working class. Argentina faced a similar situation in the early twentieth century, where its class of large landowners and industrialists feared the growth of an urban proletariat organized by left-wing parties, groups that kept increasing their share of the vote in successive elections.

Conservatives have one of two choices to make in the face of changing demography. On the one hand, they could move in an overtly authoritarian direction, and simply seize power by cancelling democratic elections or engaging in heavy-handed manipulation of electoral outcomes. German conservatives first tried to control the franchise and limit legislative power after Bismarck's unification of the country in 1871. Eventually, many German conservatives ended up throwing their support behind Hitler and his Nazi Party as an alternative preferable to the far left. In Argentina, conservatives backed a military *coup d'état* in 1930, the first of several that occurred over the next two generations.

British conservatives, on the other hand, reacted differently, by accepting and seeking to manage social change. It was Conservative prime minister Benjamin Disraeli who pushed the Second Reform Bill in 1867, which greatly expanded the franchise. He was denounced by fellow conservatives as a traitor to his social class. But, as Daniel Ziblatt has shown, Disraeli laid the groundwork for the subsequent Conservative domination of British politics through the remainder of the nineteenth century.[2] It turned out that the newly enfranchised voters found many other reasons to support Conservative politicians, like their emphasis on patriotism and their support for the Empire. It was conservatives who consolidated British democracy by their embrace of their society's growing class diversity and the social change on which it was based.

Contemporary American conservatives face a similar choice today. Conservative extremists have convinced themselves that violence may be the only way of protecting themselves from the left. It is very unlikely that this group will ever be able to enlist the US military in an anti-democratic seizure of power. But given the extent of gun ownership among this demographic, it is easy to anticipate outright violence becoming a continuing problem.

The far more significant threat is the overt conservative effort to restrict voting rights and manipulate elections. This began well before the November 2020 election, but has become a central concern of that party based on Donald Trump's false assertion that he was the victim of massive voter fraud. As Trump himself admitted, if every eligible American voted, "you'd never have a Republican elected in this country again."[3]

Many of the conservatives supporting this agenda have not broken in principle with the idea of democracy. They believe quite honestly that the election was stolen by the opposite party because their former president and his media allies have told them so. Rather than having authoritarian instincts, they are products of an information and media system that ratifies their prior preferences and supports it through motivated reasoning. The outcome, nonetheless, is an anti-democratic one that anticipates the need to overturn future election results, and has turned the Republican Party into an anti-democratic one.

Resort to these methods is, needless to say, not a formula for healthy politics, and it creates an existential threat to American liberal democracy. Conservatives could instead take a page out of Disraeli's playbook and embrace demographic change, recognizing that many voters could be enticed not by right-wing identity politics, but by conservative policies. The 2020 election saw many minority groups increase their support for Republican candidates; this suggests that many have reasons for voting Republican other than approval of an ethno-nationalist agenda. Many recent immigrant groups are socially conservative and continue to buy into an older version of the American dream rather than the one presented by left-wing identity politics. They could serve as the basis for a genuine conservative majority and not one that was the product of manipulation of the voting system.

This is what it would mean for conservatives to embrace classical liberal principles: they need to accept the fact of demographic diversity, and to make use of it to support conservative values that are not tied to fixed aspects of identity.

There is a parallel problem on the progressive left, in its inability to embrace the country's actual diversity. Diversity for this group refers primarily to specific types of social difference related to race, ethnicity, gender, and sexual orientation. It often does not include political diversity, or diversity of religious views if the latter are held by conservative Christians. Critical theory has erected a large intellectual structure which permits progressives to write off that entire element of society as part of a racist, patriarchal power structure that is illegitimately clinging to its former privileges. Deeply held religious beliefs on issues like abortion and gay marriage do not represent acceptable alternative understandings of important moral issues, but are merely examples of bigotry and prejudice that need to be rooted out.

Progressives for their part will have to accept the fact that roughly half the country does not agree with either their goals or their methods, and that they are very unlikely to simply overpower them at the ballot box any time soon. Conservatives need to come to terms with the country's shifting racial and ethnic mix, the fact that women will continue to occupy the fullest range of positions, both professionally and privately, and that gender roles have changed profoundly. Both sides quietly entertain hopes that a large majority of their fellow citizens secretly agree with them and are prevented from expressing this agreement only through media manipulations and false consciousness propagated by various elites. This is a dangerous dodge that allows partisans to simply wish actual diversity away. Classical liberalism is needed more than ever today, because the United States (as well as other liberal democracies) are more diverse than they ever were.

There are several general liberal principles that might help to manage these different forms of diversity. In the first place, classical liberals need to acknowledge the need for government, and get past the neoliberal era in which the state was demonized as an inevitable enemy of economic growth and individual freedom. On the contrary, for a modern liberal democracy to work properly, there has to be a high level of trust in government—not blind trust, but a trust borne out of recognition that government serves critical public purposes. In the United States today, we are at a point where citizens entertain the most bizarre conspiracy theories about the ways in which their government is being manipulated by shadowy elites to take away their rights, and are arming themselves in anticipation of the moment when they will have to defend themselves against the state by force. Fear and loathing of the state has existed on the left as well: many believe that the state has been captured by powerful corporate interest groups, that the CIA and National Security Agency are continuing to surveil and undermine the rights of ordinary citizens, and that the police are there primarily to enforce white privilege. Both sides tend to dismiss government as incompetent, corrupt, and illegitimate.

The urgent issue for liberal states does not have to do with the size or scope of government, which the left and right have been fighting over for decades. The issue rather is the quality of government. There is no way around the need for state capacity—that is, a government that has sufficient human and material resources to provide necessary services to its population. A modern state needs to be *impersonal*, meaning that it seeks to relate to citizens on an equal and uniform basis, and not on the basis of personal, political, or family ties to politicians wielding power at a given moment. Modern states have to deal with a whole range of complex policy issues, from macroeconomic policy to health to electromagnetic spectrum regulation and weather forecasting, and they need access to well-educated professionals with a strong sense of public purpose if they are to do their jobs well.

Liberal states have been very successful in delivering long-term economic growth, but aggregate GDP growth cannot be seen as the sole measure of success. The distribution of that growth, and the maintenance of a degree of income and wealth equality, is important for both economic and political reasons. If inequality grows too extreme, aggregate demand stagnates, and political backlash against the system grows. The idea of wealth or income redistribution has been anathema to many liberals, but the fact is that all modern states redistribute resources to greater or lesser degrees. The task is to set social protections at a sustainable level, where they do not undercut incentives and can be supported by public finance on a long-term basis.

A further liberal principle is to take federalism (or in European terms, subsidiarity) seriously, and to devolve power to the lowest appropriate levels of government. Many ambitious federal policies in areas like health care and environment were rolled out in the expectation that there would be uniform implementation of them at a state level. Taking federalism seriously means devolution to lower levels of government on a wider range of issues and allowing those levels to reflect the choices of citizens. While it may be more desirable to have common standards apply in policy areas like health or environment, democratic self-government should take precedence over uniformity of application, however desirable that may be. In general, states, counties, and municipalities have to deal with immediate problems like trash collection and policing, and therefore tend to be more pragmatic in their approaches. One of the major issues in American politics in recent years is the way that these local levels have been infected with the polarization that exists at a national level, a process that has impeded their ability to respond to local conditions.

There are, however, certain state-level decisions that do actually challenge fundamental constitutional rights and affect the basic character of liberal democracy itself. "States' rights" was the banner under which slavery and later Jim Crow were defended, and the federal government played a critical role in forcing states to accept the legal equality of African Americans. This issue is, unfortunately, returning in American politics. Republican legislatures in many states have passed or proposed bills that would effectively make it possible to overturn the results of democratic elections and make it harder to vote, especially for African Americans. The right to vote is unquestionably guaranteed in the Constitution's Fifteenth Amendment. Voting rights are fundamental rights that need to be defended by the power of the national government.

A third general liberal principle that needs to be followed is the need to protect freedom of speech, with an appropriate understanding of the limits of speech. Freedom of speech is threatened by governments, which continue to be the appropriate locus of concern. But it can also be threatened by private power, in the form of media organizations and internet platforms that artificially amplify certain voices over others. The appropriate response to this is not direct state regulation of the speech of these private actors, but rather the prevention of large accumulations of private power in the first place, through antitrust and competition laws.[4]

Liberal societies need to respect a zone of privacy surrounding each individual. Privacy is a necessary condition promoting democratic deliberation and compromise, required if individuals are ever expected to be honest about their views. It is also an outgrowth of the liberal principle of tolerance. In recognition of a society's actual diversity, citizens do *not* owe each other uniformity of thought. This is the principle underlying the US Constitution's First Amendment, as well as the free speech rights enshrined in other basic laws around the world. Yet in the United States, the federal government has come perilously close in recent years to regulating not just the sexual behavior of young people, but the way that they think about sexuality itself.[5]

Speech, and in particular public speech, needs nonetheless to be governed by a host of norms, some promulgated by the state, and others much better enforced by private entities. While liberal societies will disagree on final ends, they cannot function if they fail to agree on basic facts and to reverse their slide into epistemic relativism. There are well-established techniques for determining factual information, techniques that have been used for years in court proceedings, professional journalism, and in the scientific community. The fact that some of these institutions are periodically shown to be wrong or biased does not mean that they should lose their privilege as sources of information, or that any alternative view expressed on the internet is just as valid as any other. There are other necessary norms promoting civility and reasoned discourse that underpin democratic deliberation in a liberal society. Norms regarding public speech should furthermore be applied universally; the identity of the speaker should not determine what that speaker is allowed to say.

A fourth liberal principle concerns the continuing primacy of individual rights over the rights of cultural groups. This does not contradict the observations made earlier in this book about the degree to which individualism is an historically contingent phenomenon that is often at odds with natural human inclinations and faculties for social behavior. There are nonetheless several reasons why our institutions need to focus on the rights of individuals rather than those of groups.

People are never fully defined by their group memberships and continue to exercise individual agency. It may be important to understand the ways they have been shaped by their group identities, but social respect should take account of the individual choices that they make as well. Group recognition threatens not to remediate but to harden group differences. Inequality in group outcomes is a by-product of multiple interacting social and economic factors, many of which are well beyond the ability of policy to correct. Social policies should seek to equalize outcomes across the whole society, but they should be directed at fluid categories like class rather than fixed ones like race or ethnicity.

Even though individualism may be historically contingent, it has become so deeply part of the way that modern people understand themselves that it is hard to see how it gets walked back. Modern market economies depend heavily on flexibility, labor mobility, and innovation. If transactions need to take place within limited cultural boundaries, the size of markets and the kind of innovation that comes from cultural diversity will necessarily be limited. Individualism is not a fixed cultural characteristic of Western culture as alleged by certain versions of critical theory. It is a by-product of socioeconomic modernization that gradually takes place across different societies.

A final liberal principle has to do with recognition that

human autonomy is not unlimited. Liberal societies assume an equality of human dignity, a dignity that is rooted in an individual's ability to make choices. For that reason, they are dedicated to protecting that autonomy as a matter of basic rights.

But while autonomy is a basic liberal value, it is not the sole human good that automatically trumps all other visions of the good life. As we have seen, the realm of autonomy has steadily expanded over time, broadening from the freedom to obey rules within an existing moral framework, to making up those rules for oneself. But respect for autonomy was meant to manage and moderate the competition of deeply held beliefs, and not to displace those beliefs in their entirety. Not every human being thinks that maximizing their personal autonomy is the most important goal of life, or that disrupting every existing form of authority is necessarily a good thing. Many people are happy to limit their freedom of choice by accepting religious and moral frameworks that connect them with other people, or by living within inherited cultural traditions. America's First Amendment was meant to protect the free exercise of religion, and not to protect citizens *from* religion.

Successful liberal societies have their own culture and understanding of the good life, even if that vision may be thinner than those offered by societies bound by a single religious doctrine. They cannot be neutral with regard to the values that are necessary to sustain themselves as liberal societies. They need to prioritize public-spiritedness, tolerance, open-mindedness, and active engagement in public affairs if they are to cohere. They need to prize innovation, entrepreneurship, and risk-taking if they are to prosper economically. A society of inward-looking individuals interested only in maximizing their personal consumption will not be a society at all.

Human beings are not free-floating agents capable of reshaping themselves in any way they choose; this only happens in online virtual worlds. We are limited in the first instance by our physical bodies. Technology has done a lot to free people from the constraints imposed by their physical natures. It has liberated people from backbreaking physical labor, vastly increased life spans, overcome many forms of disease and disability, and multiplied the experiences and information that each one of us is able to process. Some techno-libertarians imagine a future in which we could each become a completely disembodied consciousness that can be uploaded into a computer, allowing us to in effect live forever. Our experience of the world is increasingly mediated by screens that allow us to easily imagine ourselves in alternative realities or as alternative beings.

The real world, however, continues to be different: wills are embedded in physical bodies that structure and also limit the extent of individual agency. It is not clear that most people want to be liberated from their own natures. Our individual identities remain rooted in the physical bodies that we are born with, and in the interactions of those bodies with the environment in which we live. Who we are as individuals is the product of the interaction of our conscious minds and physical bodies, and the memories of those interactions over time. The emotions we experience are rooted in our experience of our physical bodies. And our rights as citizens are built upon the need to protect both those physical bodies *and* our autonomous minds.

A final general principle for a liberal society would borrow a page from the playbook of the ancient Greeks. They had a saying, μηδεν αγαν (*mēden agan*), which meant "nothing in excess," and they regarded σοφροσυνη (*sophrosunē*), or "moderation," as one of their four cardinal virtues. This emphasis on moderation has been largely discarded in modern times: university graduates are routinely told to "follow their passions," and people who live to excess are criticized only when it harms their physical health. Moderation implies and requires self-restraint, the deliberate effort *not* to seek the greatest emotion or the fullest accomplishment. Moderation is seen as an artificial constraint on the inner self, whose full expression is said to be the source of human happiness and achievement.

But the Greeks may have been on to something, both with regard to individual life, and in politics. Moderation is not a bad political principle in general, and especially for a liberal order that was meant to calm political passions from the start. If the economic freedom to buy, sell, and invest is a good thing, that does not mean that removing all constraints from economic activity will be even better. If personal autonomy is the source of an individual's fulfillment, that does not mean that unlimited freedom and the constant disrupting of constraints will make a person more fulfilled. Sometimes fulfillment comes from the acceptance of limits. Recovering a sense of moderation, both individual and communal, is therefore the key to the revival—indeed, to the survival—of liberalism itself.

Notes

Preface

1. Deirdre McCloskey, *Why Liberalism Works: How True Liberal Values Produce a Freer, More Equal, Prosperous World for All* (New Haven, CT: Yale University Press, 2019).

2. See *Freedom in the World 2021: Democracy Under Siege* (Washington, DC: Freedom House, March 2021), which downgrades the freedom scores of both the US and India in 2020; Larry Diamond, "Facing Up to the Democratic Recession," *Journal of Democracy* 26 (2015): 141–55.

3. See, for example, Edmund Fawcett, *Liberalism: The Life of an Idea* (Princeton, NJ: Princeton University Press, 2014); Helena Rosenblatt, *Lost History of Liberalism* (Princeton, NJ: Princeton University Press, 2018); Larry Siedentop, *Inventing the Individual: The Origins of Western Liberalism* (London: Allen Lane, 2014); John Gray, *Liberalisms: Essays in Political Philosophy* (London and New York: Routledge, 1989).

4. Edward Luce, *The Retreat of Western Liberalism* (New York: Atlantic Monthly Press, 2017); Timothy Garton Ash, "The Future of Liberalism," *Prospect* (December 9, 2020).

5. Francis Fukuyama, "Liberalism and Its Discontents," *American Purpose* (October 3, 2020).

1. What Is Classical Liberalism?

1. John Gray, *Liberalism* (Milton Keynes, UK: Open University Press, 1986), p. x.

2. See "Vladimir Putin Says Liberalism Has 'Become Obsolete'" in the *Financial Times* (June 27, 2019), www.ft.com/content/670039ec-98f3-11e9-9573-ee5cbb98ed36

3. See Csaba Tóth, "Full Text of Viktor Orbán's Speech at Báile Tuşnad (Tusnádfürdő) of 26 July 2014," *The Budapest Beacon* (July 29, 2014).

4. Francis Fukuyama, *The Origins of Political Order: From Prehuman Times to the French Revolution* (New York: Farrar, Straus and Giroux, 2011); *Political Order and Political Decay: From the Industrial Revolution to the Globalization of Democracy* (New York: Farrar, Straus and Giroux, 2014).

5. See the examples given in Dominic J. Packer and Jay Van Bavel, *The Power of Us: Harnessing Our Shared Identities to Improve Performance, Increase Cooperation, and Promote Social Harmony* (New York and Boston: Little, Brown Spark, 2021).

6. For an account of this process, see Fukuyama (*Political Order and Political Decay*, 2014), chapter 28.

7. McCloskey (2019), p. x.

8. James Madison, Federalist No. 10 "The Same Subject Continued: The Union as Safeguard Against Domestic Faction and Insurrection," *Federalist Papers* (Dublin, OH: Coventry House Publishing, 2015).

9. For a summary, see Stephan Haggard, *Developmental States* (Cambridge, MA, and New York: Cambridge University Press, 2018); and Suzanne Berger and Ronald Dore, *National Diversity and Global Capitalism* (Ithaca, NY: Cornell University Press, 1996).

2. From Liberalism to Neoliberalism

1. For an overview of this period, see Binyamin Appelbaum, *The Economists' Hour: False Prophets, Free Markets, and the Fracture of Society* (Boston: Little, Brown, 2019).

2. Quoted in Niall Ferguson, *Doom: The Politics of Catastrophe* (New York: Penguin Press, 2021), p. 181.

3. See Branko Milanovic, *Global Inequality: A New Approach for*

the Age of Globalization (Cambridge, MA: Belknap/Harvard University Press, 2016).

3. The Selfish Individual

1. Douglass C. North, *Institutions, Institutional Change, and Economic Performance* (New York: Cambridge University Press, 1990).

2. See Deirdre N. McCloskey, *Bourgeois Dignity: Why Economics Can't Explain the Modern World* (Chicago, IL: University of Chicago Press, 2010), chapters 33–36; also McCloskey, *Beyond Positivism, Behaviorism, and Neo-Institutionalism in Economics* (Chicago, IL: University of Chicago Press: 2021, forthcoming), chapter 8.

3. Robert H. Bork and Philip Verveer, *The Antitrust Paradox: A Policy at War with Itself* (New York: Free Press, 1993); and "Legislative Intent and the Policy of the Sherman Act," *Journal of Law and Economics* 9 (1966): 7–48.

4. See Oren Cass, *The Once and Future Worker: A Vision for the Renewal of Work in America* (New York: Encounter Books, 2018).

5. Thomas Philippon, *The Great Reversal: How America Gave Up on Free Markets* (Cambridge, MA: Belknap/Harvard University Press, 2019).

6. Francis Fukuyama, "Making the Internet Safe for Democracy," *Journal of Democracy* 32 (2021): 37–44.

7. Friedrich A. Hayek, *Law, Legislation and Liberty* (Chicago, IL: University of Chicago Press, 1976).

8. See Elinor Ostrom, *Governing the Commons: The Evolution of Institutions for Collective Action* (Cambridge: Cambridge University Press, 1990).

9. Xiao-qiang Jiao, Nyamdavaa Mongol, and Fu-suo Zhang, "The Transformation of Agriculture in China: Looking Back and Looking Forward," *Journal of Integrative Agriculture* 17 (2018): 755–64, p. 757; Food and Agricultural Organization of the United Nations, www.fao.org/home/en

10. Mancur Olson, *The Logic of Collective Action: Public Goods*

and the Theory of Groups (Cambridge, MA: Harvard University Press, 1965).

11. See Siedentop (2014).

12. Fukuyama (*The Origins of Political Order*, 2011), chapter 16.

4. The Sovereign Self

1. John Rawls, *A Theory of Justice. Revised Edition* (Cambridge, MA: Belknap/Harvard University Press, 1999).

2. For a multifaceted critique of Rawls, see Allan Bloom, "Justice: John Rawls Versus the Tradition of Political Philosophy," in *Giants and Dwarves: Essays 1960–1990* (New York: Simon and Schuster, 1990).

3. Robert Nozick, *Anarchy, State, and Utopia* (New York: Basic Books, 1974).

4. Alasdair MacIntyre, *After Virtue* (Notre Dame, IN: University of Notre Dame Press, 1981), pp. 244–55; Charles Taylor, *Sources of the Self: The Making of the Modern Identity* (Cambridge, MA: Harvard University Press, 1989), pp. 88–90; Michael Walzer, *Spheres of Justice: A Defense of Pluralism and Equality* (New York: Basic Books, 1983); Michael J. Sandel, *Liberalism and the Limits of Justice. Second Edition* (New York: Cambridge University Press, 1998).

5. Sandel (1998), p. 177.

6. Ibid., pp. 179, 186.

7. J. G. A. Pocock, *The Machiavellian Moment: Florentine Political Thought and the Atlantic* (Princeton, NJ: Princeton University Press, 1975).

8. This is noted in William A. Galston, "Liberal Virtues," *American Political Science Review* 82 (1988): 1277–90.

9. Robert D. Putnam and David E. Campbell, *American Grace: How Religion Divides and Unites Us* (New York: Simon and Schuster, 2010), p. 83.

10. Abraham H. Maslow, "A Theory of Human Motivation," *Psychological Review* 50 (1950).

11. On the secular decline of trust in the United States, see Ethan

Zuckerman, *Mistrust: Why Losing Faith in Institutions Provides the Tools to Transform Them* (New York: W. W. Norton, 2020), p. 83.

12. Tara Isabella Burton, *Strange Rites: New Religions for a Godless World* (New York: PublicAffairs, 2020).

13. One of the critiques of Rawls's assertion that all people behind the veil of ignorance would choose a rule that did not disadvantage the weakest is that it assumes a very low level of risk tolerance. It is entirely possible that someone may choose to risk being badly off if he or she could also hope to become very rich and powerful—preferring a life in, say, Renaissance Italy to modern Switzerland, as in the film *The Third Man*.

5. Liberalism Turns on Itself

1. Herbert Marcuse, *One-Dimensional Man: Studies in the Ideology of Advanced Industrial Society* (Boston, MA: Beacon Press, 1991).

2. Herbert Marcuse, *Repressive Tolerance* (Berkeley, CA: Berkeley Commune Library, 1968). See also Robert Paul Wolff, *A Critique of Pure Tolerance* (Boston, MA: Beacon Press, 1965).

3. Herbert Marcuse, *Eros and Civilization: A Philosophical Inquiry into Freud* (New York: Vintage Books, 1955).

4. John Christman, *The Politics of Persons: Individual Autonomy and Socio-Historical Selves* (Cambridge, MA, and New York: Cambridge University Press, 2009), p. 2.

5. Charles W. Mills, *Black Rights/White Wrongs: The Critique of Racial Liberalism* (New York: Oxford University Press, 2017), p. 139.

6. Ann Cudd, *Analyzing Oppression* (New York: Oxford University Press, 2006), p. 34.

7. Carole Pateman, *The Sexual Contract. 30th Anniversary Edition, with a New Preface by the Author* (Stanford, CA: Stanford University Press, 2018), pp. 93–94.

8. Pateman (2018), p. 94.

9. Charles W. Mills, *The Racial Contract* (Ithaca, NY: Cornell

University Press, 1997). See also Charles W. Mills and Carole Pateman, *Contract and Domination* (Cambridge: Polity Press, 2007).

10. Samuel Moyn, "The Left's Due—and Responsibility," *American Purpose* (January 24, 2021).

11. Frantz Fanon, *The Wretched of the Earth* (New York: Grove Press, 2004).

12. Kenneth Pomeranz, *The Great Divergence: China, Europe, and the Making of the Modern World Economy* (Princeton, NJ: Princeton University Press, 2000).

13. See Pankaj Mishra, "Bland Fanatics," in *Bland Fanatics: Liberals, Race, and Empire* (New York: Farrar, Straus and Giroux, 2020).

14. Ta-Nehisi Coates, *Between the World and Me* (New York: Spiegel and Grau, 2015).

15. See Carl Schmitt, *Political Theology: Four Chapters on the Concept of Sovereignty* (Chicago, IL: University of Chicago Press, 2006).

16. Mills (1997), p. 10.

6. The Critique of Rationality

1. Peter Pomerantsev, *Nothing Is True and Everything Is Possible: The Surreal Heart of the New Russia* (New York: PublicAffairs, 2014).

2. Jonathan Rauch, *The Constitution of Knowledge: A Defense of Truth* (Washington, DC: Brookings Institution Press, 2021).

3. Alan D. Sokal and Alan Bricmont, *Fashionable Nonsense: Postmodern Intellectuals' Abuse of Science* (New York: Picador, 1999), chapter 4.

4. Theodor W. Adorno and Max Horkheimer, *Dialectic of Enlightenment* (New York: Continuum, 1982); Michel Foucault, *The Order of Things: An Archaeology of the Human Sciences* (New York: Vintage Books, 1994 [1970]).

5. Ferdinand de Saussure, *Course in General Linguistics* (New York: Columbia University Press, 2011).

6. Jacques Derrida, *Of Grammatology* (Baltimore, MD: Johns Hopkins University Press, 2016).

7. Michel Foucault, *Madness and Civilization: A History of Insanity in the Age of Reason* (New York: Vintage Books, 2013); *Discipline and Punish: The Birth of the Prison* (New York: Vintage Books, 1995); *The History of Sexuality: An Introduction* (New York: Vintage Books, 2012).

8. Edward Said, *Orientalism* (New York: Random House, 1978).

9. Kimberlé Crenshaw, "Mapping the Margins: Intersectionality, Identity Politics, and Violence against Women of Color," *Stanford Law Review* 43 (1991): 1241–99.

10. Joseph Heinrich, *The WEIRDest People in the World: How the West Became Psychologically Peculiar and Particularly Prosperous* (New York: Farrar, Straus and Giroux, 2020).

11. Luce Irigaray, "Le Sujet de la science est-il sexue? (Is the subject of science sexed?)," *Hypatia* 2 (1987): 65–87.

12. See Michel Foucault, "Right of Death and Power Over Life," in *The Foucault Reader* (New York: Pantheon Books, 1984).

13. Daniel T. Rodgers, *Age of Fracture* (Cambridge, MA: Belknap/Harvard University Press, 2011), pp. 102–107.

14. See Sokal and Bricmont (1999) for numerous examples.

15. Ibrahim X. Kendi, *How to Be an Antiracist* (London: One World, 2019); Robin DiAngelo, *White Fragility: Why It's So Hard for White People to Talk About Racism* (Boston, MA: Beacon Press, 2020).

16. Ross Douthat, "How Michel Foucault Lost the Left and Won the Right," *New York Times* (May 25, 2021).

17. See Geoff Shullenberger, "Theorycells in Trumpworld," *Outsider Theory* (January 5, 2021).

7. Technology, Privacy, and Freedom of Speech

1. In the Czech Republic, billionaire prime minister Andrej Babis became the owner of the country's largest publishing house and other media properties. In Romania, the leading TV news station was owned by billionaire Dan Voiculescu, while Slovakia's main

independent newspaper was sold to an investment group that had been the target of its investigations. See Rick Lyman, "Oligarchs of Eastern Europe Scoop Up Stakes in Media Companies," *New York Times* (November 26, 2014).

2. Martin Gurri, *The Revolt of the Public and the Crisis of Authority in the New Millennium* (San Francisco, CA: Stripe Press, 2018).

3. Jonathan Haidt, *The Righteous Mind: Why Good People Are Divided by Politics and Religion* (New York: Pantheon, 2012); Packer and Van Bavel (2021).

4. Reeve T. Bull, "Rationalizing Transparency Laws," *Yale Journal on Regulation Notice & Comment* (September 30, 2021); Lawrence Lessig, "Against Transparency: The Perils of Openness in Government," *The New Republic* (October 19, 2009); Albert Breton, *The Economics of Transparency in Politics* (Aldershot, UK: Ashgate, 2007).

5. See the account by Joe Pompeo, "'It's Chaos': Behind the Scenes of Donald McNeil's *New York Times* Exit," *Vanity Fair* (February 10, 2021).

6. The US Supreme Court found a "right to privacy" embedded in the US Constitution in *Roe v. Wade*, but used this primarily to legalize abortion and not to protect the general privacy of information or communications.

7. Adrienne LaFrance, "The Prophecies of Q," *The Atlantic* (June 2020).

8. See Richard Hofstadter, *The Paranoid Style in American Politics* (New York: Vintage, 2008).

9. In his book *The Order of Things*, Michel Foucault describes the cognitive approaches that prevailed through the sixteenth century, prior to the rise of Bacon's modern natural science. People believed that similarity, propinquity, repetition, and analogy revealed relationships between the visible world and a hidden order that was its mirror, a world that was structured by a higher power. Observers looked for signatures embedded in observed reality that provided clues to the hidden world. To understand

that world, one had to know how to read scattered signs, rather than making mental models of observed reality. In many ways, people in the internet age have retreated to this pre-scientific mode of cognition: QAnon conspiracy theorists look to scattered clues that point them in the direction of a massively different reality from the apparent one, a reality that has been manipulated by hostile elites and untrustworthy institutions. Or they look within themselves to undercover their feelings, and not to the external world that may disappoint their hopes and expectations. Foucault (1970), chapter 2.

8. Are There Alternatives?

1. Sohrab Ahmari, "Against David French-ism," *First Things* (May 29, 2019).
2. Adrian Vermeule, "Beyond Originalism," *The Atlantic* (March 31, 2020).
3. Yoram Hazony, *The Virtue of Nationalism* (New York: Basic Books, 2018).
4. Patrick J. Deneen, *Why Liberalism Failed* (New Haven, CT: Yale University Press, 2018), chapter 3.
5. Glenn Ellmers, "'Conservatism' Is No Longer Enough," *American Mind* (March 24, 2021).
6. Vermeule (2020). See also Laura K. Field, "What the Hell Happened to the Claremont Institute?" *The Bulwark* (July 13, 2021).
7. Yoram Hazony, *The Virtue of Nationalism* (New York: Basic Books, 2018).
8. Deneen (2018), chapter 3; Rod Dreher, *The Benedict Option: A Strategy for Christians in a Post-Christian World* (New York: Sentinel, 2017), chapter 1.

9. National Identity

1. See "Francis Fukuyama: Will We Ever Get Beyond the Nation-State?" *Noema Magazine* (April 29, 2021).
2. See Francis Fukuyama, "Why National Identity Matters," in Eric M. Uslaner and Nils Holtug, *National Identity and Social*

Cohesion (London and New York: Rowman and Littlefield, 2021).

3. See Hazony (2018); Rauch (2021); Matthew Yglesias, "Hungarian Nationalism Is Not the Answer," *Slow Boring* (August 6, 2021).

4. See, for example, Seymour Martin Lipset, *American Exceptionalism: A Double-Edged Sword* (New York: W. W. Norton, 1995).

5. Hazony (2018).

6. Michael Shara, *The Killer Angels* (New York: Ballantine Books, 1974), p. 27.

7. Richard Schlatter, ed., *Hobbes's Thucydides* (New Brunswick, NJ: Rutgers University Press, 1975), pp. 131–32.

10. Principles for a Liberal Society

1. See Fukuyama (2014).

2. Daniel Ziblatt, *Conservative Parties and the Birth of Democracy* (New York: Cambridge University Press, 2017).

3. Spoken on *Fox & Friends* (March 30, 2020).

4. One way of reducing the power of the internet platforms over political speech is to create a competitive layer of "middleware" companies to which curation of content can be outsourced: Francis Fukuyama, "Making the Internet Safe for Democracy," *Journal of Democracy* 32 (2021): 37–44.

5. R. Shep Melnick, *The Transformation of Title IX: Regulating Gender Equality in Education* (Washington, DC: Brookings Institution Press, 2018).

Bibliography

Appelbaum, Binyamin. *The Economists' Hour: False Prophets, Free Markets, and the Fracture of Society.* Boston: Little, Brown, 2019.

Berger, Suzanne, and Ronald Dore. *National Diversity and Global Capitalism.* Ithaca, NY: Cornell University Press, 1996.

Bloom, Allan. *Giants and Dwarfs: Essays 1960–1990.* New York: Simon and Schuster, 1990.

Bork, Robert H., and Philip Verveer. *The Antitrust Paradox: A Policy at War with Itself.* New York: Free Press, 1993.

Breton, Albert. *The Economics of Transparency in Politics.* Aldershot, UK: Ashgate, 2007.

Bull, Reeve T. "Rationalizing Transparency Laws." *Yale Journal on Regulation Notice & Comment* (September 30, 2021).

Burton, Tara Isabella. *Strange Rites: New Religions for a Godless World.* New York: Public Affairs, 2020.

Cass, Oren. *The Once and Future Worker: A Vision for the Renewal of Work in America.* New York: Encounter Books, 2018.

Christman, John. *The Politics of Persons: Individual Autonomy and Socio-Historical Selves.* Cambridge, MA, and New York: Cambridge University Press, 2009.

Coates, Ta-Nehisi. *Between the World and Me.* New York: Spiegel and Grau, 2015.

Cudd, Ann. *Analyzing Oppression.* New York: Oxford University Press, 2006.

Bibliography

Deneen, Patrick J. *Why Liberalism Failed*. New Haven, CT: Yale University Press, 2018.

Derrida, Jacques. *Of Grammatology*. Baltimore, MD: Johns Hopkins University Press, 2018.

DiAngelo, Robin. *White Fragility: Why It's So Hard for White People to Talk About Racism*. Boston, MA: Beacon Press, 2020.

Dreher, Rod. *The Benedict Option: A Strategy for Christians in a Post-Christian World*. New York: Sentinel, 2017.

Fanon, Frantz. *The Wretched of the Earth*. New York: Grove Press, 2004.

Fawcett, Edmund. *Liberalism: The Life of an Idea*. Princeton, NJ: Princeton University Press, 2014.

Ferguson, Niall. *Doom: The Politics of Catastrophe*. New York: Penguin Press, 2021.

Foucault, Michel. *Discipline and Punish: The Birth of the Prison*. New York: Vintage Books, 1995.

———. *Madness and Civilization: A History of Insanity in the Age of Reason*. New York: Vintage Books, 2013.

———. *The Foucault Reader*. New York: Pantheon Books, 1984.

———. *The Order of Things: An Archaeology of the Human Sciences*. New York: Vintage Books, 1994 [1970].

Fukuyama, Francis, *Identity: The Demand for Dignity and the Politics of Resentment*. New York: Farrar, Straus and Giroux, 2018.

———. "Making the Internet Safe for Democracy." *Journal of Democracy* 32 (2021): 37–44.

———. *Political Order and Political Decay: From the Industrial Revolution to the Globalization of Democracy*. New York: Farrar, Straus and Giroux, 2014.

———. *The Origins of Political Order: From Prehuman Times to the French Revolution*. New York: Farrar, Straus and Giroux, 2011.

Galston, William A. "Liberal Virtues." *American Political Science Review* 82 (1988): 1277–90.

Gray, John. *Liberalism*. Milton Keynes, UK: Open University Press, 1986.

Bibliography

———. *Liberalisms: Essays in Political Philosophy*. London and
New York: Routledge, 1989.

Gurri, Martin. *The Revolt of the Public and the Crisis of Authority
in the New Millennium*. San Francisco, CA: Stripe Press, 2018.

Haggard, Stephan. *Developmental States*. Cambridge, MA, and
New York: Cambridge University Press, 2018.

Haidt, Jonathan. *The Righteous Mind: Why Good People Are
Divided by Politics and Religion*. New York: Pantheon, 2012.

Hayek, Friedrich A. *Law, Legislation and Liberty*. Chicago, IL:
University of Chicago Press, 1976.

Hazony, Yoram. *The Virtue of Nationalism*. New York: Basic
Books, 2018.

Heinrich, Joseph. *The WEIRDest People in the World: How
the West Became Psychologically Peculiar and Particularly
Prosperous*. New York: Farrar, Straus and Giroux, 2020.

Hofstadter, Richard. *The Paranoid Style in American Politics*. New
York: Vintage, 2008.

Jiao, Xiao-qiang, Nyamdavaa Mongol, and Fu-suo Zhang, "The
Transformation of Agriculture in China: Looking Back and
Looking Forward." *Journal of Integrative Agriculture* 17 (2018):
755–64.

Kendi, Ibrahim X. *How to Be an Antiracist*. London: One World,
2019.

Kesler, Charles R. *Crisis of the Two Constitutions: The Rise,
Decline, and Recovery of American Greatness*. New York:
Encounter Books, 2021.

LaFrance, Adrienne. "The Prophecies of Q." *The Atlantic* (June
2020).

Lessig, Lawrence. "Against Transparency: The Perils of Openness in
Government." *The New Republic* (October 19, 2009).

Luce, Edward. *The Retreat of Western Liberalism*. New York:
Atlantic Monthly Press, 2017.

McCloskey, Deirdre N. *Bourgeois Dignity: Why Economics Can't
Explain the Modern World*. Chicago, IL: University of Chicago
Press, 2010.

Bibliography

————. *Why Liberalism Works: How True Liberal Values Produce a Freer, More Equal, Prosperous World for All*. New Haven, CT: Yale University Press, 2019.

MacIntyre, Alasdair. *After Virtue*. Notre Dame, IN: University of Notre Dame Press, 1981.

Marcuse, Herbert. *Eros and Civilization: A Philosophical Inquiry into Freud*. New York: Vintage Books, 1955.

————. *One-Dimensional Man: Studies in the Ideology of Advanced Industrial Society*. Boston, MA: Beacon Press, 1991.

————. *Repressive Tolerance*. Berkeley, CA: Berkeley Commune Library, 1968.

Maslow, Abraham H. "A Theory of Human Motivation." *Psychological Review* 50 (1950).

Melnick, R. Shep, *The Transformation of Title IX: Regulating Gender Equality in Education*. Washington, DC: Brookings Institution Press, 2018.

Milanovic, Branko. *Global Inequality: A New Approach for the Age of Globalization*. Cambridge, MA: Belknap/Harvard University Press, 2016.

Mills, Charles W. *Black Rights/White Wrongs: The Critique of Racial Liberalism*. New York: Oxford University Press, 2017.

————. *The Racial Contract*. Ithaca, NY: Cornell University Press, 1997.

Mishra, Pankaj. *Bland Fanatics: Liberals, Race, and Empire*. New York: Farrar, Straus and Giroux, 2020.

North, Douglass C. *Institutions, Institutional Change, and Economic Performance*. New York: Cambridge University Press, 1990.

Nozick, Robert. *Anarchy, State, and Utopia*. New York: Basic Books, 1974.

Nyamdavaa Mongol, Xiao-qiang Jiao, and Fu-suo Zhang. "The Transformation of Agriculture in China: Looking Back and Looking Forward." *Journal of Integrative Agriculture* 17 (2018): 755–64.

Olson, Mancur. *The Logic of Collective Action: Public Goods and the Theory of Groups*. Cambridge, MA: Harvard University Press, 1965.

Ostrom, Elinor. *Governing the Commons: The Evolution of Institutions for Collective Action*. Cambridge: Cambridge University Press, 1990.

Packer, Dominic J., and Jay J. Van Bavel. *The Power of Us: Harnessing Our Shared Identities to Improve Performance, Increase Cooperation, and Promote Social Harmony*. New York and Boston: Little, Brown Spark, 2021.

Pateman, Carole. *The Sexual Contract. 30th Anniversary Edition, with a New Preface by the Author*. Stanford, CA: Stanford University Press, 2018.

———., and Charles W. Mills. *Contract and Domination*. Cambridge: Polity Press, 2007.

Philippon, Thomas. *The Great Reversal: How America Gave Up on Free Markets*. Cambridge, MA: Belknap/Harvard University Press, 2019.

Pocock, J. G. A. *The Machiavellian Moment: Florentine Political Thought and the Atlantic*. Princeton, NJ: Princeton University Press, 1975.

Pomerantsev, Peter. *Nothing Is True and Everything Is Possible: The Surreal Heart of the New Russia*. New York: PublicAffairs, 2014.

Pomeranz, Kenneth. *The Great Divergence: China, Europe, and the Making of the Modern World Economy*. Princeton, NJ: Princeton University Press, 2000.

Putnam, Robert D., and David E. Campbell. *American Grace: How Religion Divides and Unites Us*. New York: Simon and Schuster, 2010.

Rauch, Jonathan. *The Constitution of Knowledge: A Defense of Truth*. Washington, DC: Brookings Institution Press, 2021.

Rawls, John. *A Theory of Justice. Revised Edition*. Cambridge, MA: Belknap/Harvard University Press, 1999.

Rodgers, Daniel T. *Age of Fracture*. Cambridge, MA: Belknap/Harvard University Press, 2011.

Bibliography

Rosenblatt, Helena. *Lost History of Liberalism*. Princeton, NJ: Princeton University Press, 2018.

Said, Edward. *Orientalism*. New York: Random House, 1978.

Sandel, Michael J., *Liberalism and the Limits of Justice. Second Edition*. New York: Cambridge University Press, 1998.

———. "The Procedural Republic and the Unencumbered Self." *Political Theory* 12 (1984): 81–96.

Saussure, Ferdinand de. *Course in General Linguistics*. New York: Columbia University Press, 2011.

Schmitt, Carl. *Political Theology: Four Chapters on the Concept of Sovereignty*. Chicago, IL: University of Chicago Press, 2006.

Shara, Michael. *The Killer Angels*. New York: Ballantine Books, 1974.

Siedentop, Larry. *Inventing the Individual: The Origins of Western Liberalism*. London: Allen Lane, 2014.

Sokal, Alan D., and Alan Bricmont. *Fashionable Nonsense: Postmodern Intellectuals' Abuse of Science*. New York: Picador, 1999.

Vermeule, Adrian. "Beyond Originalism." *The Atlantic* (March 31, 2020).

Walzer, Michael. *Spheres of Justice: A Defense of Pluralism and Equality*. New York: Basic Books, 1983.

Wooldridge, Adrian. *The Aristocracy of Talent: How Meritocracy Made the Modern World*. New York: Skyhorse Publishing, 2021.

Ziblatt, Daniel. *Conservative Parties and the Birth of Democracy*. New York: Cambridge University Press, 2017.

Zuckerman, Ethan. *Mistrust: Why Losing Faith in Institutions Provides the Tools to Transform Them*. New York: W. W. Norton, 2020.

Index

Page references for notes are followed by n.

Index

Index

Index

Index

Index

Index

Index